T0343794

'Fr Kevin evokes vividly the landscape and context of the fourteenth century English mystics, and with gentleness and some wit directs us to follow in their footsteps through "the hill country of the spirit". This is an enticing book, full of practical directives for us to make of our own lives a spiritual pilgrimage to the heavenly Jerusalem in the company of Walter Hilton, Julian and many other mothers and fathers of the English way.'

The Revd Canon Dr Alison Milbank, Associate Professor of Literature and Theology at the University of Nottingham, author of *The Once and Future Parish*

'Come and see. Walter Hilton is not only a mystic to admire from afar, a static representative of a certain sort of English spirituality, but a surefooted trail guide for those yet at the beginning of the way, on the foothills of the spiritual path. While armchair travellers will be edified, this book is for the rucksack rather than the coffee table, addressed to those urged on by a perhaps-inexplicable longing, shoes tied, staves in hand, ready to set off for Jerusalem. And to set out, not across some generic or idealized terrain but across the specific landscape of their own life circumstances. This book is, above all, an invitation from Walter Hilton and his four near contemporaries to come apprentice to the spiritual craft, to feel the heft of their tools, and their edge. Whatever the reader may do to keep body and soul together, they too may become learners in the kingdom of heaven, and brave the grit, grace and beauty of the way.'

The Revd Sr Hilary Crupi, OJN, Prioress of the Order of Julian of Norwich

'We're invited to become friends with these great mystical companions in order to make our own pilgrimages; whether activist or contemplative, especially devout or just travellers on the way. Here is rich fayre more than sufficient for transformative journeys.'

The Very Revd David Monteith, Dean of Canterbury

'By writing in the vernacular English of his day, Walter Hilton sought to bring the mystical tradition to a wide-ranging audience. In much the same spirit, Kevin Goodrich employs a conversational tone to invite spiritual seekers to pursue the contemplative journey, enriched by the wisdom of Hilton and his contemporaries. Goodrich has contributed to the present resurgence of interest in spirituality by directing his readers to the rich legacy of fourteenth-century English mysticism.'

The Revd Dr Julia Gatta is the Bishop Frank A. Juhan Professor of Pastoral Theology in the School of Theology, the University of the South, Sewanee, author, *The Pastoral Art of the English Mystics*

'The English mystics are a rich treasure and deep well of spiritual wisdom that deserve to be better known. Kevin Goodrich's *A Pilgrimage of the Heart* is an excellent introduction to these saints of the church. Because the Christian life is a pilgrimage, we need capable guides and the English mystics are excellent leaders. But more importantly, Goodrich is an excellent guide to these guides so that we can get to know them well, entrusting ourselves to their guidance. There is a lot of practical and helpful advice in this book that will benefit all who read it on pilgrimage.'

The Revd Dr Greg Peters, Professor of Medieval and Spiritual Theology in the Torrey Honors College, Biola University; and the Servants of Christ Research Professor of Monastic Studies and Ascetical Theology at Nashotah House Theological Seminary; author, *The Monkhood of All Believers: The Monastic Foundation of Christian Spirituality*

'I rarely read books without laying them down for a few days or weeks to return to them.

Pilgrimage of the Heart by Father Goodrich is one that I picked up and without opening another book, finished reading. As a reader with a keen interest in biographies, spirituality, and mysticism, *Pilgrimage of the Heart* not only captured my attention but also deepened my passion for real-life stories that are practical and reflective of everyday life. The book weaves the experiences of great mystics into a narrative that is not just inspiring, but also applicable to our own spiritual journeys. This is a small, easy-to-read book on prayer, contemplation, and pilgrimage. A great resource for study groups or anyone with an interest in these topics.'

The Rt Revd Jos Tharakan, Bishop of Idaho

'*A Pilgrimage of the Heart* is a true gift for anyone on a spiritual journey toward a deeper relationship with God and each other. Whether you're a spiritual director, training to be a spiritual director, or you are just searching for more, this book is for you! Father Kevin, in his beautifully inclusive ecumenical way, invites us to enter into the fullness of what God desires for each of us, reminds us that we are not meant to walk this journey alone, shows us the importance of contemplative spiritual practices in the midst of our daily lives, and introduces us to mystics that have walked this path before us and continue to light the way.'

Heidi Lender, Executive Director, Christos Center for
Spiritual Formation

A Pilgrimage of the Heart

Walter Hilton
AND THE English Mystical Tradition
Kevin Goodrich OP

DARTON · LONGMAN + TODD
INTELLIGENT ◆ INSPIRATIONAL ◆ INCLUSIVE
SPIRITUAL BOOKS

First published in 2024 by
Darton, Longman and Todd Ltd
Unit 1, The Exchange
6 Scarbrook Road
Croydon CR0 1UH

ISBN 978-1-915412-13-3

A catalogue record for this book is available from the British Library.

Cover icon and interior illustrations by Iconographer Magdalene Grace Deane

Designed and produced by Judy Linard

Printed and bound in Great Britain by Short Run Press, Exeter

I dedicate this book to my mother,
Patricia Ann Goodrich,
who in her final weeks of life,
while dealing with many troubles,
encouraged me to finish this book.

Faith is not the clinging to a shrine
but an endless pilgrimage of the heart.

ABRAHAM JOSHUA HESCHEL

CONTENTS

ↄ

INTRODUCTION

THERE'S GOLD IN THEM THAR HILLS

Evelyn Underhill, the great English spiritual director of the twentieth century, in a letter to the then Archbishop of Canterbury, Cosmo Gordon Lang, wrote, 'The interesting thing about religion is God.' As a child growing up in New England, I was more interested in the doughnuts served after worship than I was God. Further motivating my participation were all the kids at church, some of them became my good friends. Around eight years old, I began to help with the Sunday services celebrated according to the Book of Common Prayer. As an acolyte, an altar server, you had to wear a white robe. While I may have looked like a little angel, my behaviour out of the robes (and occasionally in them when the priest was not looking) was often more devilish than angelic. When I entered my teens, my principal interest in church changed from doughnuts to divinity.

God was the interesting thing about religion after all. My interest became encountering the mysterious, the luminous, and the divine. This desire to experience the truths of faith whet my appetite for all things spiritual. This quickly brought me beyond the boundaries of the Christian faith into other religions and forms of spiritual practice. Several of which seemed to take spirituality more seriously based on my limited experience with Christianity at the time. The pilgrimage, the journey of my life, was a mess of spiritualities, ideologies, and experiences. I ventured down trails marked and unmarked, trails authorized and unauthorized by parents and church authorities. Eventually, during the hustle and bustle of all this spiritual experimentation I encountered an unusual group of people, the Christian mystics and monastics.

Monastics are those who take vows to follow Christ in community. Mystics are individuals who enjoy a special closeness with God. Walter Hilton, the fourteenth-century monastic and mystic, is the primary historical guide to the spiritual life in this book. As a young adult, Hilton was not someone I knew about. At the time, I was just beginning to learn about one of his contemporaries, Julian of Norwich, who we will meet later. The monastics and mystics revealed to me that there was veritable gold, spiritual treasure, hidden in the hills of the Christian faith. Looking back, it is hard to see how I missed this wealth of wisdom that was before my eyes in every service and beckoning my heart in every silent prayer. But as J. R. R. Tolkien wrote in his novel, *The Lord of the Rings,* 'all that is gold does not glitter'.

Guidance for Seeking and Finding

The morning was still. The air, chill. The leaves on the shadowed trees were brittle and bent, their colours rustic reds and browns. Fall's glory was fading fast on the late November landscape. Dawn revealed a sky with barely a cloud, displaying a vast canvas of blue. Straight ahead, far into the distance, were rolling hills. The Ozarks in northern Arkansas have a rugged beauty to them. I was on my annual retreat—a silent retreat. Besides a cat, I had the small retreat centre to myself. This included a simple chapel dedicated to Saint Francis of Assisi. The chapel offered a tremendous view of the countryside through glass windows stretching from floor to ceiling. I beheld hundreds of autumn-accented hills. The spiritual life is like those hills. It is full of valleys, streams, forests, and rugged terrain. It is full of secrets, perils, and possibilities.

C. S. Lewis, one of the most influential Christian writers of the twentieth century, did not consider himself to be a mystic.

He considered mysticism as the highest point of prayer, as 'the crags up which mystics vanish out of sight'. While Lewis may not have been a mystic, he knew about them. Responding to a letter from Father Bede Griffiths, asking him whether he had read Walter Hilton's book, *The Scale of Perfection,* Lewis replied, 'Yes, I've read it with much admiration.' In his autobiography, *Surprised by Joy,* recalling a time early in life when his faith was failing, Lewis wrote, 'If only someone had read me old Walter Hilton's warning that we must never in prayer strive to extort by mastery what God does not give.' Lewis recognized in Hilton a spiritual wisdom. A wisdom not limited to the highest hilltops of prayer, but wise also to the ordinary foothills of the Christian experience. Over the centuries, women and men of all sorts and conditions, like Lewis, have read Hilton with admiration. They have discovered in him and the wider English Mystical Tradition inspiration and insight for navigating the landscape of faith.

Hilton and the other English mystics of the fourteenth century form a holy fellowship. A fellowship we can join. We join them not only by reading them but by making our own journeys, like they did, into the hill country of the Spirit. Like them, we can seek treasures, too. The treasures of the God experience. We can seek and find the gift of God's golden love poured into our hearts. A sense of connection to something larger than our life's immediate concerns. Without guidance, we risk unnecessary setbacks. With guidance, we gain companions for the journey's ascents and descents. Even with others cheering us on, the way will still sometimes be hard. Yet, it will be a far richer life of pilgrimage, of transformation, than if we attempted the journey on our own. Hilton writes of this mystical quest, 'The searching is wearisome but the finding is glorious.'

Illumination Over Information

This book is something of a trail guide to the valleys, foothills, and mountain vistas of the spiritual life according to the teachings of the English Mystical Tradition. It is a book intended for those who want not only to learn concepts about the life of faith but who desire to live a life of faith. Those who desire to do more than go through the motions of religion, but to embrace the relationship at the heart of religion. To answer Jesus' invitation to 'Come and see' (John 1:39). To experience a faith that illuminates the hidden path like a torch in the dark of the night. A faith that warms the spirit like a hot cup of tea after coming in from a freezing rain. Walter Hilton will serve as our guide in this exploration, pointing us toward the contemplative treasures offered to us by God.

You will learn a bit about history, theology, and spirituality in this book, including spiritual concepts and practices. You will learn about different mystics, saints, teachers, and writers. Some of these individuals we will linger with, but most we will quickly pass by. This dynamic mirrors our experience of the twists and turns of our lives. Some people travel with us for a short interval. There are others who because of blood, affection, or common situations weave in and out of our lives for long stretches. All are fellow travellers on the path to God. Yet, more than places and practices, dates and doctrines, my prayer is that you will learn something about yourself through these pages. Self-knowledge is a necessary prerequisite for growing in God knowledge. Hilton wrote to individuals so they might grow in the knowledge and love of God. This book shares in that purpose, knowing other purposes will be helped along the way.

In the Middle Ages, works of theology and spiritual direction were generally written in Latin. This was changing in the fourteenth century. Hilton wrote in the vernacular, in what we now call Middle English. He was accessible, which partially accounts for his popularity as a spiritual writer. In that spirit, I have used modern translations of Hilton, and the other English mystics' works. I have occasionally edited the translations or rendered my own translation, after consulting the Middle English and where applicable, the Latin. At the end of each chapter, I have included a section called next steps. These sections include questions for individual or group reflection. I have also included exercises for implementing the chapter's ideas, as well as optional side trips. The appendices include a recommended reading list, suggestions for using the book in a variety of settings, and several other helps. Finally, I have limited the number of endnotes to make this work as accessible as possible. With God's help, let us begin.

CHAPTER ONE

STARTING THE JOURNEY

'The trouble is that we live far from ourselves and
have but little wish to get any nearer to ourselves.'
The Way of the Pilgrim

Starting the Journey

I'd missed the plane. This meant that the kindly couple who had agreed to pick me up from the East Midlands airport in England would be inconvenienced. It also meant that my small window of opportunity to make pilgrimage to the priory church of St Peter in Thurgarton was even smaller. My first encounter with Walter Hilton was during a graduate course on Anglican spirituality at Nashotah House, a seminary in Wisconsin in the United States. Everyone in the class was a priest or training to be one. That class was several years behind me on that day I missed the plane. At Nashotah, Hilton's warm and insightful guidance drew my interest. After the course, he remained on my shelf, seldom, if ever, coming down. Now, years later, as I pursued further study and research, Hilton came off the shelf and back into my life. Here was my opportunity to make pilgrimage to his church – a pilgrimage being a journey to a sacred place for a sacred purpose – and I'd missed the plane.

The delay was disappointing, but I wasn't that far away. I was in Dublin, Ireland, and I'd be able to arrive in England the next morning. I remember seeing the signs for the village of Thurgarton

A PILGRIMAGE OF THE HEART

as the taxi driver brought me a few miles up the road to the market town of Southwell. Southwell and Thurgarton were both significant church centres in the fourteenth century. In the Church of England, a minster is a designation for a church, usually of some architectural significance, that at one point in its history housed a monastic community – a community of monks or nuns. The Minster church in Southwell is centuries old, rich with history, and active in faith. It serves as the Cathedral for the Anglican diocese of Southwell and Nottingham. The ruins of the archbishop's palace are adjacent to the Minister. The visitors to Southwell over the centuries include Cardinal Wolsey in 1530, just after his failure to secure a divorce for King Henry VIII from Catherine of Aragon. Monarchs have visited the Minster too. King Richard the Lionheart in 1194 and Queen Elizabeth II in 1984. I love the Minster and have enjoyed returning there many times over the years.

My anticipation on this first trip to the lands of Hilton focused on the small village just four miles south of Southwell, Thurgarton. There Hilton entered the Augustinian priory and wrote his most influential works. I stayed at Sacrista Prebend, a retreat house, across from the Minster. I was taken through the eighteenth-century home, passing the various rooms, each named after a saint. My heart smiled when I got to my room, the name on the door was none other than Walter Hilton. Sacrista and the Minster community have done much to preserve the witness of Walter Hilton, their local saint, and for this I am most grateful. Taking the bus or a car would make for a quick journey to Thurgarton. I'd already resolved, however, to make the pilgrimage the old-fashioned way, by foot.

The lands surrounding Southwell and Thurgarton are largely farmland. Not unlike what they may have been like in the time of Hilton. The countryside is full of gently rolling hills, well-cultivated fields, and miles of well-marked paths. It was May, and the landscape was green as I set out from the retreat house to the village of Thurgarton. Like many a pilgrim before me, I chose to make my own way, assuming I'd be able to sort out which paths to take. This didn't work as well as I had planned. I moved off the paved motorway with its twists and turns and attempted to walk alongside the road. The underbrush was too thick for this in many spots. I got turned around somehow, stopped in the middle of some farmer's field, and realized I'd gone off in the wrong direction. The spiritual life can be like this. I should have procured a map of the walking trails or asked for directions in Southwell. On this journey, however, I was blessed. Eventually, more than an hour later, I saw the signs for the village of Thurgarton.

On the way to the priory church there is a paved walkway along a narrow road that rises up a hill. After all these years of studying Hilton, I was about to arrive at the church where he lived, ministered, and died. I arrived at the gate to the churchyard, taking in the sight of the impressive priory church, one of the original two towers, still stretching high above. The door was left open, a gracious gesture by the local churchwarden. No one else was there. Just the saints that had gone before and a palpable sense of centuries of prayer saturating the space down to the old foundation stones. I entered with a sense of quiet awe. There is a memorial to Hilton on one of the stone pillars. It dates from 1996 when they celebrated the 600th anniversary of Hilton's death. Parts of the existing church go back to the time of Hilton and even before. The church has high ceilings, stunning stained glass, and an altar that is believed to be of medieval vintage. It was surreal to be in the same church where Hilton and the other Augustinian priests gathered for prayer and the celebration of the Eucharist, Holy Communion. Just outside of the priory, at the time of this writing, you can see fields with grazing sheep. A sight Hilton probably enjoyed as well.

Invitation Accepted

This book is an invitation for readers to make their life a pilgrimage and go beyond wandering the hills of the Spirit to resolutely, intentionally, seeking their treasures. It is also an invitation to seek out companions for the journey, past and present. Pilgrimage, a journey taken to a sacred place for a sacred purpose, was a popular devotional practice in fourteenth-century England. This is remarkable when you consider the challenge involved in travelling by foot, cart, or horseback across great distances, which were often dangerous. A journey always offers the possibility of peril, even if the journey is as brief as the distance between your home and your car. In the Middle Ages, pilgrimages often involved travelling hundreds of miles, but it has changed in recent times. The time required today to complete one of the historic pilgrimages, such as to the Holy Land, is brief in comparison to what would have taken our ancestors in the faith at least months to complete.

This book is a guide to the Christian spiritual life anchored in the witness of the fourteenth-century English Mystical Tradition. Walter Hilton will serve as our chief guide and point of reference into this tradition. Christians are always looking to the past in order to live the present and move into the future. Hilton and the other major figures of the English Mystical Tradition, Richard Rolle, the *Cloud of Unknowing* author, Julian of Norwich, and Margery Kempe lived in times distinct from ours. Learning about them allows us to situate our spiritual ancestors within their own historic challenges and circumstances. This can also provide valuable perspective on our own challenges and circumstances. A danger in looking to the past for spiritual insight is to idealize those who have gone before us and to wish our lives and our times could be like theirs. This obscures our ability to appreciate the full humanity of people from the past. This can also result in reading into their times the hopes and aspirations of our own. To a degree this is inevitable, but we better honour those who have gone before us and better receive inspiration from them if we attempt to understand them on their own terms. So then, as we begin our journey together, we will explore some of the circumstances of Walter Hilton's life and times.

STARTING THE JOURNEY

The Good Old Days

Charles Dickens begins his novel *A Tale of Two Cities*, with the line, 'It was the best of times, it was the worst of times'. Dickens' novel focuses on characters living during the nineteenth century. A novel written about the fourteenth century, the time of Hilton, might appropriately begin, 'It was the worst of times, the very worst of times'. Every century of human history has witnessed awful hardships, but the fourteenth century, especially in England, was a time of great suffering. Historians have questioned the moniker of the 'Dark Ages' as an appropriate description of the Middle Ages. The Middle Ages, roughly the period of AD 500 through to 1500, were characterized by achievements and advances, as well as by failures and regressions. Yet, the fourteenth century was without question a dark time. Large numbers of the population believed the end of the world was near. Their reasons were not so much about esoteric interpretations of Holy Scripture, but about the terrible disruptions to daily life that were happening all around them.

Horrific happenings aside, the fourteenth century was a time when medicine was limited and life expectancy was short. Upwards of half of children did not survive to adulthood. Most people did not live past fifty, though there were plenty of exceptions. Early in the century there was a great famine. Describing this time, the theologian Joan Nuth writes in her book, *God's Lovers in an Age of Anxiety*, 'Stories were told of people eating horses, dogs, and even other humans to survive; thousands starved. But this suffering was pale in comparison to what was to come.'[1] Hilton may have grown up hearing stories about this famine from his parents and relatives. He was born around 1340, possibly in Hilton, Huntingdonshire, a region about sixty miles north of London. Today this distance can be travelled in about two hours by car. In the fourteenth century, the journey would have taken considerably longer. We know almost nothing about Hilton's family or early childhood. This is not an unusual situation where medieval writers are concerned.

The bubonic plague broke out on more than one occasion

in England, killing close to half the population, as well as higher percentages of the clergy. Hilton would have been around eight years old when some of the worst outbreaks occurred. Entire villages, monasteries, and other communities were wiped out by this gruesome disease. Ghost towns were everywhere. They were constant reminders to the living that the plague, also known as the Black Death, could at any moment sweep in and destroy your entire community. Most of the population, including Walter Hilton, would have known several people who died of the plague. In some cases, these would have been close friends and family members, not only distant acquaintances. One historical commentator put it this way, 'Towns which were formerly well populated have been reduced to desert places by the death of the citizens, and in many a district in England there is not one left in a thousand nor two for ten thousand.'[2]

If famine and plague were not enough to break the human spirit and provide presumptive evidence that the end of the world was near, fourteenth-century England had additional difficulties. The Hundred Year War with France began in 1337 and continued intermittently throughout the century. This war began before Hilton was born and continued after he died. The Church, which was enmeshed in all facets of English society at this time, was troubled on multiple fronts. A major problem was a shortage of priests and other clergy because of the plague. Since clergy and monks often lived in community and frequently tended to the sick and dying, they died in greater numbers than the general population.

Theological trouble was also brewing, as an Oxford professor named John Wycliffe, along with his followers, elicited much controversy in their calls for Church reform. Hilton, who must have demonstrated an aptitude for learning as a boy, was admitted as a teenager to Cambridge University around 1355. The minimum age for admission was fourteen and it was common for those few who went to university around this age to stay several years to complete their studies. No women attended university.

STARTING THE JOURNEY

The universities were relatively new, Oxford was founded in 1096 and Cambridge in 1209. Before them, there had been and still were schools of learning centred around cathedrals and monasteries. It doesn't appear that Hilton came from a well-to-do family, which meant that his admission to Cambridge was made possible by his ability and the good graces of a patron who paid his expenses. While at Cambridge, he would have learned more about Wycliffe and his followers. In time, they were referred to as Lollards, and their movement, declared heretical by the Church, as Lollardly. The Lollards were forerunners of the Protestant reformers. While the Lollards were denounced in the fourteenth century, similar ideas and sentiments gained momentum over a hundred and fifty years later. The Protestant Reformation began in Germany in 1517, inspired by a pugnacious Augustinian priest named Martin Luther. Wycliffe questioned many of the practices of the Church, including the sacramental system of infant baptism, Holy Communion, and private confession. He argued for a Christian faith more explicitly rooted in the Bible. When Wycliffe translated the Bible into English in 1382, the Church condemned his translation.

Another trouble facing the Church was schism. Duelling popes arose in Avignon, France, and in Rome, Italy. The Church split as different bishops, dioceses, and religious orders aligned with one pope or the other. This state of division lasted for most of Hilton's life, beginning around 1309 and concluding with the restoration of a united papacy in 1376.

To make matters worse, the clergy and vowed religious often had a poor reputation among the populace. Certainly, there were exemplary priests, monks, and nuns in England during this era. Yet the overall impression conveyed by the popular literature of the time, such as Geoffrey Chaucer's *Canterbury Tales*, paints a very unflattering picture of the Church's leadership. While Chaucer includes some favourably portrayed religious characters in his story about a group of travellers on pilgrimage to Canterbury, he uses satire to critique several others. For example, a conceited nun and a swindling friar. In the friar's case, Chaucer points out how the friar prefers the company of the 'rich' and 'sellers of food' to that of, 'sick lepers' and 'paupers'. In other words, the friar is a hypocrite, ignoring his vows to serve others and instead using his position to serve himself.

Taking the Road Less Travelled

At Cambridge, Walter Hilton studied law. He was trained in the laws that pertained to the state and the laws that pertained to the Church. In fourteenth-century England, there was considerable intersection between these two sets of laws and between the governance of the King and lords, the nobility, and with the governance of the pope and bishops, the spiritual nobility. There is evidence that he practiced law in the consistory court system of the diocese of Ely. Hilton's training in law and theology gave him a secure position in society. To run the daily operations of the Church in a diocese—a region supervised by a bishop—required a whole system of laws, lawyers, ecclesiastical offices, and officers. There was also the possibility of advancement. Hilton's schoolmate from Cambridge, Adam Horsley, another lawyer, had made good progress in his career, having become an official of the Royal Exchequer. Both men began to have doubts about their commitment to the system. Each was sensing a call to a life of overt spiritual commitment and contemplation. A life that would provide little personal income and in the eyes of most, offer far less prestige.

Hilton's colleagues held a low view of those who abandoned their position in order to dedicate themselves to prayer. Hilton writes the following to Horsley:

> They believe that if you despise the world and dismiss both the study and practice of the law from your mind, cast off honours, degrees, and benefices, and choose poverty and humility for Christ's sake, that you are infatuated and insane. For they would say to you what some used to say to me, 'With your knowledge and intelligence, how well you would do in

court cases and lawsuits and such! You already know what I am talking about here, so do not be taken in by them if they try to entice you by saying, 'Come with us, all kinds of precious wealth we shall gain.' – consent not to them!'[3]

While Horsley was considering entry into a monastic community, Hilton, too, was considering his options. A life of contemplation and prayer in fourteenth-century England meant one of two pathways. The first was entry into a monastic community, like the Carthusian Order, which Horsley was considering. The second was entry into the solitary life. One of the notable elements of the English Mystical Tradition is its high regard for the solitary life. This form of Christian commitment goes back to the Desert Fathers and Mothers of the third century. In England, it came in two versions, that of the anchorite or anchoress, and that of the hermit. The substantial difference between the two was that anchoresses and anchorites were bound to one location and hermits were free to travel from location to location. Whether monk or nun, anchoress or hermit, there were established guidelines for entering into and living out these forms of Christian commitment. The most famous being the thirteenth-century, *Ancrene Wisse,*[4] a guide for anchoresses. Hilton first chose to become a hermit. While some writers of the time, such as Richard Rolle, who we will meet later, viewed the solitary life as embodying the highest ideals of the spiritual life, Hilton struggled in his new vocation. In another letter to his friend Adam Horsley, he wrote:

What are we doing, the two of us and our like, lazy and useless men standing idle all the day long? We are not labouring in the Lord's vineyard administering the sacraments, nor do we preach the word of God abroad or manifest the spiritual works of mercy. We are like children having taken leave of our senses and our will-power, we are under no rule of life.[5]

A PILGRIMAGE OF THE HEART

Hilton's concern for making a practical difference in the lives of others is interesting. Contemplative life was understood as a literal retreat from the concerns of the world to devote oneself to God. This was the vocation of the contemplative nun, anchoress, or hermit. Later, as a spiritual guide to such individuals, Hilton affirms and supports their commitments. Yet, for himself, Hilton finds a home with the Augustinian Canons, entering their priory in the village of Thurgarton around 1386, in present-day Nottinghamshire. Augustinian Canons were like monks in that they lived together in community and prayed together at intervals throughout the day, but like parish priests, they also engaged in active ministry among people. Hilton's reputation as a spiritual guide began to grow during his time as a hermit and reached its maturity during his time in Thurgarton. His own experiences with leaving the consistory court system and wrestling with his vocation gave him an understanding predisposition toward the struggles of others. His reputation as a holy man, who knew the ways of God and prayer, resulted in others seeking out his counsel. Probably a good deal of this took place in person in the village. Today, Hilton is known to us only because of his written works, some of which became widely known. These writings reveal his insightful, gentle, and flexible approach to giving spiritual guidance.

STARTING THE JOURNEY

Writings

Hilton's most influential book, written during his years at Thurgarton, is *The Scale of Perfection*. Sometimes the title is rendered the *Ladder of Perfection*. The work comprises two separate books, however, the two books are contained in one volume in most manuscripts from the medieval period and in almost all contemporary editions. The two sections of the book are complementary. The first book gives more attention to the early stages of the spiritual development and the second book gives more attention to the later stages of spiritual development. Hilton, like most of the great spiritual teachers from antiquity to the Middle Ages, recognized the spiritual life as being developmental. Based on Holy Scripture, the basic truths of the faith, and centuries of gathered experience from seekers of God, he identified sequential stages and predictable challenges as common to those pursuing a deeper spiritual life.

The two traditional theological disciplines associated with these stages, challenges, and experiences are ascetical theology and mystical theology. Later a unified understanding of these two types of theology arose called spiritual theology. Hilton is a theologian in both the ascetical and mystical senses. Ascetical has to do with the ordinary Christian life, the active life of most Christians, and the mystical, having to do with higher states of prayer, the contemplative life of a few Christians. Ascetical comes from the Greek word *askesis* meaning training or exercise. Ascetical theology gives attention to the exercises, the means, and ways that we can grow in the practice of the Christian faith. Mystical comes from the Greek word *mystikos* meaning hidden or secret. Mystical theology builds upon the ordinary Christian life outlined in ascetical theology but focuses on the hidden life of interior prayer and spirituality.

Today we would call Hilton a spiritual director. A spiritual director is a Christian, lay or ordained, man or woman, who through gifting, training, and experience provides spiritual guidance to others, usually in a one-to-one setting. Hilton was certainly a spiritual guide, but to be a spiritual director in the medieval church was to be a theologian immersed in the ascetical and mystical traditions. *The Scale* is a work of ascetical and mystical theology directed pastorally to an individual, pastoral being associated with the ministry of shepherding and guiding souls. This ancient and medieval understanding is carried into the present understanding of the pastoral work of priests, pastors, and ministers. Hilton's and the English Mystical Tradition's understanding of the purpose of theology is expressed well by the fourth-century desert monk, Evagrius Ponticus, who wrote, 'a theologian is one who prays'.

The Scale is addressed to an anchoress, a woman who has recently entered this form of Christian commitment, a form of the solitary life, with the goal of seeking and experiencing, as much as she can, union with God. Hilton begins the book in this way: 'Spiritual Sister in Jesus Christ, I beseech you to be contented in the vocation through which our Lord has called you to serve him, and in it to stand firm, toiling busily with all the powers of your soul; and by the grace of Jesus Christ to fulfil in true righteousness of living the state to which you have committed yourself.'[6]

While probably written for a particular anchoress, Hilton appears to be aware the book will have a wider audience. Regardless, *The Scale* became one of the most widely circulated books on spiritual theology in the fourteenth and fifteenth centuries. Professor Bernard McGinn, a widely attested scholar of Christian mysticism, wrote on why Hilton's book was so popular and why it has held a steady place among sources of spiritual direction over the centuries. He writes, 'Hilton provides a handbook of the whole spiritual path, from its beginnings in the grace of baptism and the sacrament of penance to the union with Christ possible in this life.'[7] Father David Knowles, in his *The English Mystical Tradition*, shares a similar sentiment, '*The Scale* is in aim a Summa of the whole spiritual life an attempt to give in outline its degrees and duties.'[8] Mother Julia Gatta in her *Three Spiritual Directors of our Time* writes, 'In the late fourteenth and fifteenth centuries, there was in England no more highly esteemed devotional writer than Walter Hilton.'[9] His book had the honour of being the first work of English mysticism to be printed. It was published by Wynkyn de Worde in 1494 at the bequest of Lady Margaret Beaufort, mother of King Henry VII.[10] McGinn adds, 'Scholars of Middle English literature have praised Hilton's prose. Among the attractive features of *The Scale* is Hilton's use of direct address, which sometimes breaks into dialogue.'[11] Hilton is a theologian, but his style in *The Scale* and other works is pastoral and personal. He isn't writing academic treatises to be read only by theological technicians but is writing spiritual guidance for all sorts and conditions of people.

Hilton's second most influential work, *The Epistle on the Mixed Life*,[12] was also written during his time at Thurgarton. It is shorter than *The Scale* and is addressed to a worldly lord, a man with significant responsibilities of governance, business, and family life. Like Hilton when he was practising law, this worldly lord was questioning what he was doing with his life. He was wrestling with a desire to pursue a life of greater spiritual commitment and contemplation. He was considering leaving his responsibilities, and presumably his family, to pursue this desire. He may have been considering entering a monastery. Such a move was not unheard of in the Middle Ages. Hilton's response was probably unexpected:

> You must not totally follow your desire to leave your business activities in the world, which are needed to organize the lives of yourself and your dependents, and to give yourself up to spiritual occupation in prayers and meditations – like a monk, a friar or any other man not bound in the world by children and servants as you are. It is not right for you, and if you do this you are not keeping to the order of charity.[13]

These are strong words from a lowly canon to a secular man of responsibility. While closing one set of doors with this advice, Hilton opens another unexpected set of doors for this man of worldly affairs. A spiritual innovation where Hilton opens the possibility of a serious spiritual life to those outside of the monastery. A possibility available to even more people today than in Hilton's time. We'll return to this innovation later

Hilton wrote other works, usually classified as minor, which reflect their brevity and their relative influence compared to his major works. He wrote *Of Angel's Song*, *Eight Chapters on Perfection* and is generally believed to have translated from Latin into the Middle English, *The Goad of Love*. In Latin he authored, *The Image of Sin (De imagine peccati)*, *The Usefulness and Prerogatives of Religious Life (De utilitate et prerogativis religionis)*, *Letter on Reading, Intention, Prayer and Meditation (Epistola de leccione, intencione, oracione, meditacione et Alis)*, *A Letter to Someone Renouncing the World (Epistola ad quemdam seculo renunciare volentem)* and *Believe Firmly (Firmissime crede)*.[14] Hilton addressed most of these Latin works to individuals reflecting his ministry as a spiritual guide and director within his own lifetime. He is sometimes credited with having written commentaries on Psalm 90 and Psalm 91 in the Vulgate version of the Bible. Also, he is sometimes cited as the author of a commentary on Benedictus, a song of praise used in the daily services of prayer based on Zechariah's utterance in Luke chapter 1.

Hilton lived during a tumultuous time. The restoration of the papacy in 1376 must have been a comfort to him, but unprecedented peasant revolts erupted only five years later. They were in response to severe taxation, due in part to the war with France. Cities were looted and government officials were murdered. Additionally, the Church continued to deal with controversies caused by the Lollards. Hilton's prior, the head of the Augustinian community in Thurgarton, was authorized to arrest Lollards. This was not a far-away problem somewhere else – it was in Hilton's backyard. The fear of the Lollards and the methods to deal with them grew increasingly severe. Hilton died on the Eve of the Annunciation of Mary, March 24, 1396.

In 1401, the severity of Lollard persecution crossed a new line when the first Lollard, William Sawtry, was sentenced to death and burned at the stake. Hilton's life had started with the promise of a Cambridge education, and the practice of law in the diocesan system, but took a radical turn when he left behind the possibilities of advancement and secure employment to seek a deeper life of prayer. First, he tried being a hermit, before becoming a canon of St Augustine at the priory church in Thurgarton. There he found his vocational stride. In that community, by God's grace, Hilton secured a lasting legacy as a theologian and spiritual director, whose writings have guided souls seeking union with Christ for centuries to the present day.

Influences

Hilton is rooted in the Bible and the teachings of the Church. While the use of the Bible by individuals was controversial in his time, Hilton sees the Bible as a valuable resource for those who can read. The controversies of the fourteenth century were not about using the Bible per se. Medieval worship services, preaching, art, culture, and architecture were full of biblical passages and references. The daily services prayed by monastics were replete with Scripture. Part of the controversy of the fourteenth century was whether the Bible should be translated into the common tongue and used widely in that language, expanding access to the Scriptures to the small but growing literate population. This would mean so-called 'ordinary' Christians would be able to read and hear the Bible for themselves and not only through the ministrations of Church authorities. The authorized Bible of the era, the Vulgate translation, was in Latin. Hilton quotes the Bible in both Latin, as well as English. For Hilton, the Scriptures are not to be avoided by individuals seeking a deeper spiritual life, but studied, and especially prayed over as a means of encountering God. In the *Scale,* Hilton, writing about the Scriptures, quotes approvingly Romans chapter fifteen verse four: 'For whatever was written in former days was written for our instruction, so that by steadfastness and by the encouragement of the scriptures we might have hope.'

Hilton did not write in a vacuum. Like all writers, especially

Christian writers, he owed his insights, teachings, and experiences to those who came before him and to those who lived around him. These were all vehicles through which the Holy Spirit operated in his life. In some cases, theologians, historians, and literature scholars can identify and trace these influences to their sources. Sometimes it is clear he's drawing upon ideas associated with the most influential theologians of his time, the fifth-century North African bishop, St Augustine of Hippo and the twelfth-century Italian Dominican friar, St Thomas Aquinas. At other times he is drawing upon the work of past Augustinian Canons, such as the spiritual writers Hugh and Richard of St Victor, from the eleventh and twelfth centuries, respectively. In other cases, when he reaches conclusions similar to other authors, it could be they are both expressing ideas that were commonplace in their time. Finally, because Hilton and other writers possessed similar backgrounds and lived at the same time, they may have come to the same conclusions independently. Later in the book, as we meet the other mystics of this era, we will see these dynamics at work

To press this point further, the heritage of a given school of Christian spirituality, such as the fourteenth-century English Mystical Tradition, can be compared to the layers of a historic church. Is the priory church of St Peter in Thurgarton, Hilton's church? Yes and no. There are architectural elements that go back to the time of Hilton. There are architectural elements that go back to the nineteenth century, and some more recent improvements. It has served as a church, a place of prayer and praise, for centuries, but during this duration it has undergone renovation, deterioration, and reconstruction.

In some cases, you can point to parts of the building and identify which are from the fourteenth century or the nineteenth century. In other cases, the materials from different centuries have blended together. This is not unlike Hilton when he communicates ideas that other teachers of the faith communicated before him. Sometimes you can say an idea of Hilton's is similar too and probably came from St Bernard of Clairvaux, a twelfth-century monk whose writings influenced much subsequent spiritual writing in the Middle Ages. In other cases, Hilton tells us his source such as when he quotes the seventh-century bishop, St Gregory the Great. At other times, when reading a medieval spiritual writer, you cannot be certain of an idea's origin. You can only be certain that Hilton, and the other mystics we're exploring in this book, are embodying, faithfully and sometimes creatively, the long tradition of Christian asceticism and mysticism that preceded them. Sometimes these influences will be pointed out in our journey together, but sometimes they will not. In this way, Walter Hilton will remain our primary historical guide and point of reference into the English Mystical Tradition.

Constant Turmoil: A Theology of Love

Fourteenth-century England was a difficult century. It was an era of great disruption, death on a terrible scale, constant war, and controversy. Many thought the end of the world was near and that the 'Black Death' was a sign of God's judgment. Many felt that God was no longer listening and that in effect, God had abandoned them to their sin. In *Piers Plowman*, a fourteenth-century allegorical poem, we get a sense of how many felt during those awful times:

> Since the time of the plague, friars and frauds like them have been dreaming up difficulties as a diversion for the sneering upper classes. Out of sheer clerical bloody-mindedness they deliver sermons at the cross outside of St Paul's, the effect of which is to undermine people's faith, so that they cease to give generous alms or feel sorry any longer for their sins. In the religious orders, and indeed in all sections of society, rich and poor alike, pride has reached such proportions that prayers have lost all efficacy as a means of stopping the plague. These days, God seems to be deaf – he can't even be bothered to open his ears.

This belief was voiced not only by common people but by many preachers and teachers of the Church. Some of what they preached added to the terror of the age. A remarkable characteristic of Walter Hilton and the other figures of the English Mystical Tradition is their theology of hope in a loving God. In the face of massive death and disruption, they spoke of a warmth and consolation that could be experienced through union with God. This was not a rosy, just be happy, always look on the bright side of life, attitude. Such an attitude was impossible to hold in the face of so much death and destruction. Their attitude was one of faith, bathed in grace, and strengthened by their experience of the love of God through the mystic path. A good test of a spirituality is its endurance in the face of suffering. Perhaps this is why Hilton has endured throughout all these centuries because his words were not written against the backdrop of an idyllic time of peace and health but against the backdrop of a time of war and plague. Whatever wars or plagues we face, outside our doors, or inside our hearts, we can turn with Walter Hilton toward the warm fire of God's love. We can begin to make our way to Jerusalem.

NEXT STEPS

- Make your life a pilgrimage
- Learn about one or more of these topics on your own:
  Black Death   100 Years War   Spiritual Direction
  Lollardy   Mystical Theology   Contemplation
  Ascetical Theology
- Have a cup of tea.

PRAY

The Collect for Purity

STARTING THE JOURNEY

'Almighty God, to you all hearts are open, all desires known, and from you no secrets are hid: Cleanse the thoughts of our hearts by the inspiration of your Holy Spirit, that we may perfectly love you, and worthily magnify your holy Name; through Christ our Lord.'

The Book of Common Prayer

EXERCISES

Choose one or more exercises to enrich and deepen your learning from this chapter.

- *Map It*

  Look up Thurgarton and Nottinghamshire on the map. Get a sense of where Thurgarton is in relation to London, Jerusalem, and your own location. How long would it take you to travel to London, Jerusalem, and Thurgarton?

- *Seek and Find*

  Choose a historical topic, piece of literature, or individual from this chapter and do some informal and relatively brief research. For example, you could look up more information on the bubonic plague, Chaucer's *Canterbury Tales*, or on the number of Minster Churches in the Church of England.

- *Prepare For Pilgrimage*

  One of the purposes of this book is to invite readers to make their lives a pilgrimage. Brainstorm on your own or with others how someone might prepare to go on a specific pilgrimage, say to Thurgarton, and how these preparations might relate metaphorically or literally to how an individual might make their entire life a pilgrimage.

QUESTIONS

For individual or group reflection.

1. Prior to learning about this book and reading this chapter

had you ever heard of Walter Hilton or the English Mystical Tradition? If so, when, and how? If not, have you ever heard of the words, mystic, and mysticism? When you read or hear these words what associations, ideas, or people come into your mind?

2. What is a pilgrimage? Do you know anyone who has ever been on a pilgrimage? Have you ever thought of going on a pilgrimage yourself? If you could make a pilgrimage anywhere in the world, where would you go?

3. What are your impressions of fourteenth-century England? Would you have enjoyed living during this time period? Do you see any parallels or points of contact between then and now?

4. Who was Walter Hilton? What are some things we know about him? What are your first impressions about him as a human being and as a spiritual guide?

5. The author writes, 'A good test of a spirituality is its endurance in the face of suffering.' Do you agree with this statement? Why or why not?

SIDE TRIP

I travell'd on, seeing the hill, where lay
My expectation.
A long it was and weary way.
The gloomy cave of Desperation
I left on th' one, and on the other side
The rock of Pride.

And so I came to fancy's meadow strow'd
With many a flower:
Fain would I here have made abode,
But I was quicken'd by my hour.
So to care's copse I came, and there got through
With much ado.

STARTING THE JOURNEY

That led me to the wild of Passion, which
Some call the wold;
A wasted place, but sometimes rich.
Here I was robb'd of all my gold,
Save one good Angell, which a friend had ti'd
Close to my side.

At length I got unto the gladsome hill,
Where lay my hope,
Where lay my heart; and climbing still,
When I had gain'd the brow and top,
A lake of brackish waters on the ground
Was all I found.

With that abash'd and struck with many a sting
Of swarming fears,
I fell, and cry'd, Alas my King!
Can both the way and end be tears?
Yet taking heart I rose, and then perceiv'd
I was deceiv'd:

My hill was further: so I flung away,
Yet heard a crie
Just as I went, None goes that way
And lives: If that be all, said I,
After so foul a journey death is fair,
And but a chair.

George Herbert (1593-1633), *The Pilgrimage*

CHAPTER TWO

KNOWING THE DESTINATION

'The Spirit calls me there, and I must go.'

Sojourner Truth

The Way to Jerusalem

Throughout the Bible, Jerusalem is prominent. In the Old Testament, it is the capital city of Israel, the location of the Great Temple. It is the city of kings and the political, social, and religious centre of the nation. In the New Testament, it is a captured capital under the rule of the Roman Empire, a constant reminder to the people they are an occupied nation. Jerusalem is also the setting for Jesus' passion, the final days before his death. In the Gospel of Luke, Jesus' turning toward Jerusalem is a decisive moment. 'When the days drew near for him to be taken up, he set his face to go to Jerusalem' (Luke 9:51). His ministry of preaching, teaching, and healing in rural Galilee is coming to an end. The culminating events of his earthy life—betrayal, arrest, suffering, and death on a cross—are about to begin. In the Gospel of Matthew, Jesus, surrounded by his disciples, laments, 'Jerusalem, Jerusalem, the city that kills the prophets and stones those who are sent to it! How often I have desired to gather your children together as a hen gathers her brood under her wings, and you were not willing!' (Matthew 23:27).

In *The Scale of Perfection*, Hilton offers his reader a parable about a pilgrim desiring to go to Jerusalem. It begins like this:

A PILGRIMAGE OF THE HEART

There was a man wanting to go to Jerusalem and because he did not know the way he came to another man who he thought knew it and asked whether he could reach the city. The other man told him he could not get there without great hardship and labour, for the way is long and the perils are great, with thieves and robbers as well as many other difficulties to beset a man on his journeys; also there are many different ways seeming to lead in that direction, yet people are being killed and robbed daily and cannot come to the place they desire. However, there is one way, and he would undertake that anyone who takes and keeps to it shall come to the city of Jerusalem, and never lose his life or be slain or die of want. He would often be robbed and badly beaten and suffer great distress on his journey, but his life would always be safe. Then the pilgrim said: 'If it is true that I can keep my life and come to the place I desire, I do not care what trouble I suffer on the journey, and therefore tell me what you will, and I promise faithfully to do as you say.' The other man answered and said this: 'See, I am setting you on the right road. This is the way and be sure to keep the instructions I give you.'[15]

According to the man who possesses the knowledge of the right road to Jerusalem, the way is difficult and will certainly involve suffering. With the assurance of arriving at his destination, the pilgrim is willing to suffer robbery and beating. I'd be inclined, where I am the pilgrim in the parable, to ask if there was another way to Jerusalem that did not involve being robbed and beaten! No such option is offered. We will return to the man's guidance to the pilgrim regarding the right road.

Jerusalem, the city where Jesus suffered and died and where Jesus was raised and glorified is the paradigmatic pilgrimage destination of the Christian faith. The earliest observances in that city commemorating the events of Jesus' passion are hidden from us. We don't know exactly when they began or what they first looked like. They may have started as early as the first year after Jesus' resurrection. How soon Christians beyond the immediate region began to travel to Jerusalem to celebrate these events is also unknown. However, as the Christian Church expanded and her forms of prayer and liturgy developed, devotion and travel to the Holy Land grew. Pilgrims travelled there year-round. They went to the places associated with Jesus' ministry, his death, and resurrection. They also visited places associated with the Old Testament. Egeria, a pilgrim to Jerusalem in the late-fourth century, writes the following in her journal: 'When everyone arrives at Gethsemane, they have an appropriate prayer, a hymn, a reading from the Gospel about the Lord's arrest. By the time it has been read everyone is groaning and lamenting and weeping so loud that people even across the city can probably hear.'[16]

Hers is but one of the earliest accounts, which history has added to in great numbers, from across the globe and the centuries. Ten centuries later, during the time of Hilton, pilgrimage to Jerusalem and other holy sites had become a major devotional practice for people of all social classes across the Christian world, including England. Guidebooks for pilgrims were produced in great numbers. For example, the twelfth-century work, *The Pilgrim's Guide to St James of Compostela.* Santiago de Compostela is in Spain and it's associated with St James the Apostle. It has seen a tremendous resurgence as a place of pilgrimage in recent years, but was also a major pilgrimage destination in the Middle Ages.

Sites were made holy by their association with saints and then over time, by the number of pilgrims who visited the saint's shrine, offering their prayers, and worshipping God in that place. People made pilgrimages for numerous reasons, sometimes to seek healing for themselves, healing for a loved one, as an act of thanksgiving for answered prayer, or as a form of penance for a notorious sin. A natural desire to see new places was certainly an underlying factor in some cases. However, unlike the modern curiosity and impulse to travel felt by so many people today, the knowledge that medieval travel was long, difficult, and dangerous tempered any desire to travel. You might not return and probably knew people, or of people, who hadn't returned from a business trip, pilgrimage, or military campaign. It wasn't a rare tragedy, but part and parcel of living in the fourteenth century. Pilgrimage always involved peril, whatever benefits it provided. This is also true of spiritual pilgrimage; a serious pursuit of the journey of faith will always involve dangers.

Besides Jerusalem, Hilton and his contemporaries had many other options. Some of them were closer to home, such as the pilgrimage to Canterbury Cathedral and the shrine of St Thomas Becket. In 1595, William Shakespeare's play, *King Richard II*, immortalized on stage the murder of Archbishop Becket in 1170. The monarch's infamous words, 'Who will rid me of this meddlesome priest?', apparently uttered in frustration and not intended as an order, inspired knights to murder Becket, a close confidant of the king. There was also the pilgrimage to the shrine to the Blessed Mother, St Mary, in Walsingham. The Christian world in the Middle Ages venerated Mary, and England had a particular reputation for Marian devotion. Another local option was the pilgrimage to St Alban's, the shrine of England's first martyr. Alban was a layman and a new convert to Christianity who in the fourth century saved the life of a priest hiding from persecution. People still go on pilgrimages to these places today. The Church's practice of granting indulgences - the forgiveness of sins derived from the merits of the saints - was part of the spiritual and material economy of pilgrimage in the medieval ages. Hilton's early training in canon law, the laws of the church, probably included the subject of indulgences. However, he gives no attention to this practice in any of his known writings. Another form of measurement given to pilgrimages was their spiritual value relative to making a pilgrimage to Jerusalem.

For example, it was said that two pilgrimages to the shrine of St David in Wales was equivalent to making one pilgrimage to Rome, and three pilgrimages to St David's equalled one pilgrimage to Jerusalem. Pilgrims had to be fed and housed. On popular pilgrimage routes, there arose whole networks of support services in the form of inns, churches, and monasteries. For longer pilgrimages, like the one from England to the Holy Land, there were ships and guides offering the medieval equivalent of all-inclusive tours to holy sites. Travel cost a lot of money back then, as it does now. Wealthier travellers could afford their own accommodation, but those with fewer means relied on the hospitality of monasteries and shared accommodation, often with strangers, sleeping in a common area. People usually travelled in groups in medieval England, as it was dangerous to travel alone. Groups afforded some measure of safety from thieves and other hostiles. There are lessons here for the spiritual life.

You Can Get to Jerusalem Before you Get to Jerusalem
It was November. It was cold back home, but in Jerusalem the weather was sunny and comfortable. People were all around me, most of them wearing modern clothes, and while we took a bus that morning through very modern traffic, my excitement was not for the comforts of modern Israel but for the ancient site we were approaching. Our group of pilgrims, of which I was the youngest, began to separate, the men going one way and the women the other. The sound of prayer in Hebrew could be heard. We were at the great Western Wall in the old city of Jerusalem—also known as the Western Wailing Wall. It is the only remnant of the Temple not destroyed by the Romans in AD 70. The Temple that would have been known to Jesus and his followers. The same Temple that Jesus visited as a boy, 'they found him in the temple, sitting among the teachers, listening to them and asking them questions' (Luke 2:49). It's also where he visited later as a popular, if controversial, rabbinic teacher and prophet, 'And all the people would get up early in the morning to listen to him in the temple' (Luke 21:38). The Temple was where Jesus, 'drove out those who were selling

and those who were buying in the temple' and declared 'Is it not written, "My house shall be called a house of prayer for all the nations", but you have made it a den of robbers' (Mark 11:15, 17). Today the wall is sacred to Jews, Christians, and Muslims.

To approach the wall, you must be dressed somewhat conservatively by Western standards. As a man, you have to cover your head out of respect for God. You've probably seen a Jewish man somewhere, perhaps in the airport, wearing a kippah. They look similar to the white, red, purple, and black skull caps worn by some Christian priests, most notably the Pope. (I have one. It's not white in case you were wondering.) The wall is about fifty feet high and a hundred and fifty feet long. When I was there, you could see hundreds of paper notes in the crevices of the wall. There were letters, prayer requests, and private communications to God. Written in many languages, pilgrims from around the world had placed these notes. I was a novice brother in the Dominican order at the time, not yet a priest, and green with enthusiasm to be in the Holy Land. There was a spiritual presence and power at the wall. As I closed my eyes and put my hand where hundreds of thousands of pilgrims had put their hands, I experienced a sense of the holy.

I felt a connection that superseded time and place. This space was heavy with the impressions of over 2000 years of prayer, worship, and emotion. That moment at the wall has stayed with me, even though other parts of that pilgrimage have faded from my memory. Thinking back to the parable, does this mean I realized the high point of the spiritual life before I had ever read a single word of Walter Hilton? After all, I found a way to Jerusalem that didn't involve being robbed or beaten. (Okay. So, an Israeli customs officer at the airport gave me a verbal ribbing, but I don't think that counts.) Finding the right road to Jerusalem is relatively easy. Save the money, book the ticket, and get yourself on a plane. Alternatively, take Highway 1 from Tel Aviv to get there by car. We don't need to hear the rest of the parable, right? We have figured out a modern workaround. Actually, I discovered, as generations of spiritual seekers before me have, that it is quite possible to get to Jerusalem before getting to Jerusalem.

A Pilgrimage of the Heart

Pilgrimage was popular in Hilton's time. So popular that Hilton uses pilgrimage as an analogy, a teaching device, for the spiritual life. Hilton explains, 'According to our spiritual proposition, Jerusalem is as much as to say sight of peace and stands for contemplation in perfect love of God, for contemplation is nothing other than a sight of Jesus, who is true peace. Then if you long to come to this blessed sight of true peace and to be a faithful pilgrim toward Jerusalem. I shall set you on the way that leads toward it.'[17] In the *Scale of Perfection*, Hilton is giving guidance to an anchoress. Her goal and call were to seek union with God through prayer. In Hilton's time, people understood contemplation as part of the highest stages of prayer where an individual could experience the presence of God in a powerful and personal way. Contemplation was understood as a prayerful union with the Triune God involving a profound awareness of God's presence. Contemplation was a work of grace and a gift of God. Yet, the individual could prepare themselves to receive what only God could give. This was a pilgrimage of the heart. It remains a pilgrimage of the heart today. Some manuscripts, instead of using the word scale, ladder, or perfection, give Hilton's book the title, *The Way of Contemplation.*

The pilgrimage spirituality of Walter Hilton implies a faith that is going somewhere. This is a faith that brings us to different places, that grows over the years, and that will involve twists and turns on the road to Jerusalem. Pilgrimage spirituality implies that growth in Christ takes time and will sometimes involve setbacks and sufferings. Such a faith is about more than being a good person or attending a church. This is a faith, a Christianity, of the heart and the spirit. It isn't an easy spirituality; it is a rigorous spirituality. It is challenging faith, but challenging in a way that is akin to becoming a better parent, spouse, or friend. Hilton, and the other writers of the English Mystical Tradition, are far more concerned that we grow in our love of God and neighbour than in our love for particular bits of information. Their interest is our transformation.

More accurately, their interest is in the contemplation of God – the sight, experience, and love of God. To experience these realities as a human being is to be transformed. Contemplation is not navel-gazing but receiving the loving gaze of God. Contemplation is a journey of ten thousand steps that can be taken in stillness. In *Soul Travel: Spiritual Journeys in Late Medieval and Early Modern Europe*, historians Jennifer Hillman and Elizabeth Tingle summarize well the place of pilgrimage in the Christian faith:

> The Christian tradition has at its core, a spiritual journey. The Passion of Jesus, written in the texts of the Gospels as a narrative through Jerusalem, from Gethsemane to Golgotha, was relived in the mind of every reader and listener from the first century onwards. Almost as early is the tradition of the Christian as a pilgrim, a traveller to places made holy by Christ and his apostles, then by his martyrs and confessor saints. Christians were also allegorical pilgrims, journeying through life from birth to the celestial kingdom.[18]

A Heavenly City Accessible on Earth

The final chapter of the book of Revelation, which is the final chapter of the Bible, describes a new heaven and a new earth, complete with a new Jerusalem:

> Then I saw a new heaven and a new earth; for the first heaven and the first earth had passed away, and the sea was no more. And I saw the holy city, the new Jerusalem, coming down out of heaven from God, prepared as a bride adorned for her husband. And I heard a loud voice from the throne saying, 'See, the home of God is among mortals. He will dwell with them as their God; they will be his peoples, and God himself will be with them; he will wipe every tear from their eyes. Death will be no more;

mourning and crying and pain will be no more, for the first things have passed away.' And the one who was seated on the throne said, 'See, I am making all things new.'

Also, he said, 'Write this, for these words are trustworthy and true.' Then he said to me, 'It is done! I am the Alpha and the Omega, the beginning and the end' (Revelation 21:1-6).

Over the centuries the Christian mystics have witnessed to the reality of this city, but not only as a hope for a distant future, but as a city, a spiritual reality, that can be experienced now. Not fully, not completely, but a city that can be beheld by faith. A city that can be experienced in prayer, through the grace of God in contemplation. This has been the experience of the Christian mystics. This is the spiritual Jerusalem. This is an analogy for experiencing and entering into the deep reality of the Trinity. A reality known and experienced through Jesus Christ in the power of the Holy Spirit. This is a spirituality of intimacy, of knowing God, as a mother knows her child by holding her to her breast. This is a spirituality where God finds a home in our hearts. A spirituality where we can sit by the crackling fire of contemplation with God. Even those graced and called to a life of contemplation cannot always remain by this fire. They will experience periods where the fire wanes and they will have to go in search of kindling. They will experience periods where they must attend to their needs and those around them. There is more to the pilgrimage of the heart than stillness.

There is action, too. There is the climbing of the steep hill of character transformation. There is stopping by the wayside to help our neighbour on the side of the road. There is life with all its glorious highs, crushing lows, and sometimes tedious day-to-day responsibilities. This too can be part of making your life a pilgrimage. Instead of limiting spirituality to occasional visits to the splendid shrines hidden in the hills, include it all. The muddy pathways, the cold nights, the sometimes-irritating travel companions, and the sometimes less-than-inspiring worship services of your local church—all can be parts of the pilgrimages of our lives. It is a journey with and toward God. For Hilton and the other writers of the English Mystical Tradition, there is a right road to this spiritual Jerusalem. This road is available to those who long to arrive at the heavenly city. Heaven is not only a future state, a destination to be hoped for only past the mysterious gates of death, but is a reality, the mystics teach us, that can begin to be experienced now. Saint Catherine of Siena, an Italian contemporary of the English mystics, phrased this truth pithily, 'All the way to heaven is heaven.'

Climbing the Ladder of Perfection

In many medieval and modern manuscripts, Hilton's most influential work, The Scale of Perfection is alternatively titled The Ladder of Perfection. This title draws upon the extensive use of ladder imagery by teachers of prayer over the centuries. For example, the influential Ladder of Divine Ascent was written by a Syrian monk, John Climacus, in the sixth century. He wrote it at St Catherine's Monastery on Mount Athos in Greece. Developing this tradition and exercising its own persuasive influence was The Ladder of Monks written by Guigo II in the twelfth century. He wrote it at the Grande Chartreuse monastery in France. Both monastic communities are active today and have been for over 1000 years. These works and others draw upon the imagery from the Book of Genesis where Jacob 'dreamed that there was a ladder set up on the earth, the top of it reaching to heaven; and the angels of God were ascending and descending on it' (Genesis 28:12). Later, Jacob wrestles with God in the form of an angel: 'Jacob was left alone; and a man wrestled with him until daybreak' (Genesis 32:24). A ladder implies an ascent upwards toward God with steps or stages to the spiritual life. Furthermore, a ladder implies our participation but as something we cannot do without assistance. The pilgrimage of the heart is a gift offered to us by God's grace.

KNOWING THE DESTINATION

We do not earn our way up the ladder. Like Jacob, as we pursue a serious spiritual life, we may find ourselves wrestling with God, our beliefs, and the difficult parts of ourselves.

All we can do is prepare to receive what God chooses to give us. We can prayerfully choose to climb the ladder. We can wilfully refuse to climb the ladder. The ladder is simply another image used to communicate the spiritual reality of pilgrimage. Faith in Christ invites movement and growth. While not intended as a literal image, the ladder invites us upward into the heart of God. Hilton, like those before him, understood the ladder as leading toward a particular kind of life, a life of perfection. The language of perfection has challenged, inspired, and discouraged Christians for centuries. The idea of perfection comes from The Sermon on the Mount (Matthew 5-7). In this sermon, Jesus vividly describes a picture of the Kingdom of God, inviting his listeners to embrace a life of radical commitment. The sermon begins like this:

Blessed are the poor in spirit, for theirs is the kingdom of heaven. Blessed are those who mourn, for they will be comforted. Blessed are the meek, for they will inherit the earth. Blessed are those who hunger and thirst for righteousness, for they will be filled. Blessed are the merciful, for they will receive mercy. Blessed are the pure in heart, for they will see God. Blessed are the peacemakers, for they will be called children of God. Blessed are those who are persecuted for righteousness' sake, for theirs is the kingdom of heaven. Blessed are you when people revile you and persecute you and utter all kinds of evil against you falsely on my account. Rejoice and be glad, for your reward is great in heaven, for in the same way they persecuted the prophets who were before you. (Matthew 5:1-12)

Later in this same sermon, Jesus says, 'Be perfect, therefore, as your heavenly Father is perfect' (Matthew 5:48). The ethically and spiritually challenging content of the Sermon on the Mount came to be understood early in Christian history as summarizing the demanding way of life that Christians accept when answering Jesus' call to follow, 'If any want to become my followers, let them deny themselves and take up their cross and follow me' (Matthew 16:24). Throughout the centuries, many have questioned the feasibility of ordinary and imperfect human beings living out the ideals of the Sermon of the Mount. Likewise, throughout the centuries, Jesus' invitation to discipleship, to be his follower or student, as expressed in the Sermon on the Mount, has inspired women and men to pursue this demanding path. Hilton, like most teachers of Christian discipleship, tells us growth in God is a never-ending project in this life. The process of growing in God is sometimes referred to as the pursuit of holiness or sanctification. Holiness means becoming whole persons created in the image of God, while sanctification is living into the sacredness of who we are and who we can become in God. This process always offers us new challenges and new vistas in this life. In other words, there will always be more rungs on the ladder of perfection to climb. Perfection in the spiritual journey is more about growing in nearness to perfection, God, than about achieving self-perfection ourselves.

The Active Life, Loving Neighbour; The Contemplative Life, Loving God

Over time, Jesus' teachings and life, including the ideals in the Sermon of the Mount, came to be associated with moral excellence and with contemplative excellence. Moral excellence is living out Jesus' commandment to love one's neighbour. Jesus is the ultimate example of living this commandment faithfully, evidenced by his compassion for so many. 'When Jesus went ashore, he saw a great crowd; and he had compassion for them and cured their sick' (Matthew 14:14). Contemplative excellence is living out Jesus' commandment to love God. Jesus is the ultimate example of living this commandment faithfully, evidenced by his close relationship with the Father, 'Jesus spent the night in prayer to God' (Luke 6:12).

KNOWING THE DESTINATION

In this way, The Sermon on the Mount and the whole of Jesus' teaching were understood as having a contemplative dimension— for example, 'Blessed are the pure in heart for they will see God' (Matthew 5:8). The Christian committed to the contemplative life is striving to cooperate with the Holy Spirit to purify their heart so that they might see God. The contemplative doesn't see God literally and fully, but by the Holy Spirit comes to know, experience, and be aware of God in all things. The Sermon on the Mount, and the whole of Jesus' teaching, were understood as having an active dimension. For example, 'Blessed are the merciful, for they will be shown mercy' (Matthew 5:7). The Christian committed to the active life is striving to cooperate with the Holy Spirit to empower them to show mercy to their neighbour. To extend care and concern, as well as practical help and assistance to others.

The active life of the Christian focuses outward. We love God through caring for our neighbours. The contemplative life of the Christian focuses inward. We also love God through prayer. Both actives and contemplatives engage in mercy to neighbour and in prayer, but most of their attention is directed to one or the other. Until Hilton's time, it was understood that the active life was for most Christians, while the contemplative life was for a few Christians. Active life was mostly for the laity. Contemplative life was mostly for solitaries and monastics. Clergy, in theory, fit somewhere in between these two categories. In practice, many clergy, unless they were also monks, lived active lives. This remains the case today. The way of perfection was only available to those who took vows to dedicate their lives to contemplation, renouncing marriage, personal possessions, and worldly responsibilities. There were exceptions over the centuries to this understanding, but this view was the predominant perspective of most theologians and spiritual directors in the Western Church.

51

A PILGRIMAGE OF THE HEART

I Want Out of the Rat Race

This background helps us to understand the predicament of the worldly lord who sought Hilton's guidance concerning his desire to set aside his active life responsibilities and pursue a life of contemplation. Hilton gives his answer to this man in his second most influential work, *The Mixed Life*. You may recall Hilton's response:

> You must not totally follow your desire to leave your business activities in the world, which are needed to organize the lives of yourself and your dependents, and to give yourself up to spiritual occupation in prayers and mediations – like a monk, a friar or any other man not bound to the world by children and servants as you are. It is not right for you, and if you do this you are not keeping to the due order of charity.[19]

The order of charity or the law of love is one of the guiding principles of Walter Hilton's spiritual direction. This law is derived from Jesus' Great Commandment, 'You shall love the Lord your God with all your heart, and with all your soul, and with all your mind.' This is the greatest and first commandment. And a second is like it: 'You shall love your neighbour as yourself' (Matthew 22:37-40).

The law of love affirms the primacy of love in the Christian life. The kind of love this law commands is not an ethereal feeling directed to no one. It is a love expressed in responsible action toward particular people. In the case of the lord, it included his family, his employees, and other dependents. Faithfulness to God on the pilgrimage to Jerusalem involves faithfulness to the people in our lives. Hilton affirms the importance of family life and work. Most Christians are called to the active life. Active life generally involves a combination of family life, friendship, work, and societal obligation. Hilton doesn't dismiss these as unimportant. He includes them in the spiritual life by situating them within the boundaries of the order of charity. If Hilton stopped there, we would still be left with considerable food for thought. His words invite each of us to include our families, friendships, relationships, work, and social responsibilities as arenas for living out our faith. As environments like gardens, where we cultivate the flowers and fruits of virtue and charity. Charity is the older English word for self-denying, Jesus-like, love. When we are discerning— prayerfully thinking through the options of our lives and the desires of our hearts—God invites us to consider them in relation to the order of charity.

Hilton could have stopped where he did. He could have encouraged the man of responsibility to dedicate himself more fully to the active life. However, Hilton does something else. After telling the man that the order of charity does not permit him to leave behind his business, children, and servants, Hilton adds, 'And so too, if you wanted to abandon all spiritual activity and concentrate entirely on the business of the world, leading the active life completely as other people who never felt the grace of devotion, you would lose the order of charity.'[20] What is the man to do? Hilton says he can't become a contemplative, leaving behind all his responsibilities. Hilton also says he can't become an active, leaving behind his inclinations toward devotion. It is here that Hilton pushes open the double doors of contemplation, a serious spiritual life of prayer and reflection, to a wider audience. He adds, 'for your position requires you to do both at different times'.[21] This is a third way to make the pilgrimage to Jerusalem. It is not the active way of pilgrimage of graced moral action or the contemplative way of pilgrimage of graced prayer, but a mix of the two. A mixed life. A life that combines elements of the active, love toward neighbour and the development of personal virtue, with elements of the contemplative, love toward God and the development of personal prayer. Hilton summarizes this combination in this way, 'You must mix the tasks of the active life with the spiritual labours of the contemplative life, and then you will do well.'[22] For centuries before Hilton, the biblical account of Jesus' visit to the home of Mary and Martha in Bethany served as an illustration of these two ways of living the Christian life:

> Now as they went on their way, he entered a certain village where a woman named Martha welcomed him. She had a sister named Mary, who sat at Jesus's feet and listened to what he was saying. But Martha was distracted by her many tasks, so she came to him and asked, 'Lord, do you not care that my sister has left me to do all the work by myself? Tell her, then, to help me.' But the Lord answered her, 'Martha, Martha, you are worried and distracted by many things, but few things are needed—indeed only one. Mary has chosen the better part, which will not be taken away from her. (Luke 10:38-42)

Jesus' explanation in this passage that 'Mary has chosen the better part' (Luke 10:42) led to a general conviction among theologians and spiritual directors of the superiority of the contemplative life over the active life. Hilton, in instructing the man of responsibility, employs this familiar usage, but as in his previous counsel, affirms the value of the active life. He states, 'For at one time you must be busy with Martha, managing and directing your household, your children, your servants, your neighbours and your tenants. Another time you must with Mary leave the activities of the world and sit down at our Lord's feet in prayer and holy thoughts, contemplating him to the grace he gives you.'[23] These words, 'the grace he gives you,' are another guiding principle of Hilton's spiritual direction. Earlier Hilton refers to 'other people who never felt the grace of devotion.'[24]

The mixed and contemplative lives are for those who have been gifted with a desire for them—a desire for a deeper spiritual life. For many, this desire might come and go. It might manifest as a sense of internal restlessness or as a desire for more than participation in the usual church committees and activities. These kinds of feelings can be extremely frustrating for people who have

KNOWING THE DESTINATION

little knowledge of or connection to Christians familiar with the contemplative tradition. They have a desire for more but don't know where to find it. This would be like a little girl naturally gifted to be a great concert pianist who has never sat down at a piano or heard one played. She may have an inclination toward music, but the popular music she's familiar with only teases her sense of inner vocation, it doesn't awaken it. Her awakening doesn't happen until she hears Beethoven's *Moonlight Sonata* played by her friend's piano teacher and then places her fingers on the keys for the first time. Then her sense of inner vocation awakens full throttle. This is her conversion. She says to herself, 'This is for me! This is what I am supposed to do! This is what I want more of!' Her desire for the piano is awakened by the music. What was dormant in her, her natural ability, needed the gift of grace, the notes given life by the strings of her friend's piano, and the skill of her friend's piano teacher. She was in no way responsible for those notes. They come into her life as a pure gift. She has done nothing to merit them or cause them to be played. Without that experience, she would remain ignorant of what she was capable of. We might say, what she was created for – to play and to feel deeply. To contemplate Bach or Mozart not as interesting musical theories, but as heavenly harmonies that reverberate through her fingers into every part of her body, mind, and soul.

This analogy speaks to the necessity of a graced desire from God to be drawn to the contemplative life. It also speaks to the necessity of the Church stewarding well its contemplative treasures, hidden in the hills of Christian history, spirituality, and practice. Stewarding them well so that those who occasionally attend a service, but are yearning for something deeper in their lives, know there is more to be found and experienced. So that those who are maxed out with activities of all kinds, including church activities, know their faith offers them more than busyness. If the Church can steward well this treasured inheritance people will know where to turn when they have a desire for a deeper spiritual experience. By participating in the Church such seekers will be able to 'hear' contemplative music for the first time. Then they too will know what they were created for, to seek and experience God deeply. Such seekers should, of course, turn to God. They also should turn to God's friends, the mystics. The mystics will then point them in the direction of the right road and accompany them along the way. With our pilgrim staffs in hand and Hilton by our side, let's round the next bend in the road to meet some of the other spiritual writers of the English Mystical Tradition.

NEXT STEPS
- Make your life a pilgrimage
- Learn about one or more of these topics on your own:
  Jerusalem   St Thomas Becket   Walsingham
  Contemplative Life   Western Wailing Wall
  St Catherine of Siena   Active Life
- Have a cup of tea.

PRAY

> The Lord's Prayer
> Our Father, who art in heaven,
> hallowed be thy name;
> thy kingdom come;
> thy will be done;
> on earth as it is in heaven.
> Give us this day our daily bread.
> And forgive us our trespasses,
> as we forgive those who trespass against us.

KNOWING THE DESTINATION

And lead us not into temptation;
But deliver us from evil.
For thine is the kingdom,
the power and the glory,
For ever and ever.
Amen.

EXERCISES

Choose one or more exercises to enrich and deepen your learning from this chapter.

- *The Stations of the Cross*
  The Stations of the Cross is a devotional practice utilizing fourteen pictures, carvings, or statues to depict events in the life of Christ from his being condemned to death, to his crucifixion and burial. Some churches have a permanent set, but it is also possible to create temporary stations. The stations can also be prayed in place, the movement happening in the imagination of the participants. You can pray the stations individually, in a small group, or in a formal service. They are an ancient way of making a spiritual pilgrimage.

- *Team Martha or Team Mary*
  Read the passage about Mary and Martha from Luke 10:38-42. Enter one of the debates of the ages by choosing your team, Martha or Mary. In choosing your team not only consider what your natural temperament is, but which team is better from your perspective. This will require you to try to make sense of what Jesus means by, 'Mary has chosen the better part.'

- *The Sermon on the Mount*
  Jesus' most powerful, influential, and explained-away sermon is found in the Gospel of Matthew, chapters five to seven. Read these chapters on your own. Take note of the verses

you find inspirational, challenging, and perplexing. In reading the sermon, see if you can discern the two threads the author highlights in this chapter, a moral thread and a contemplative thread.

QUESTIONS

1. What do you know about the city of Jerusalem? Does it play any significant role in your understanding of Christian history, faith, and imagination? If so, how and why? If not, why not?

2. What is the difference between a pilgrimage of the heart and a pilgrimage of the feet? Can you truly make a pilgrimage of the heart in place? Can you truly make a pilgrimage of the feet without your heart being moved?

3. What is the way of perfection? Does the author suggest it means achieving a state of flawless faith, without doubts, and a flawless faith, in perfect observance of God's commands? What did the way of perfection mean for Hilton and the English mystics?

4. The active life and the contemplative life were important theological concepts and spiritual distinctions in the fourteenth century. Have you heard of these two kinds of lives before? Regardless, what do you think about them, how would you define them, and do you see examples of people living these two lives today?

SIDE TRIP

> Our journey had advanced —
> Our feet were almost come
> To that odd Fork in Being's Road —
> Eternity — by Term —
> Our pace took sudden awe —
> Our feet — reluctant — led —
> Before — were Cities — but Between —
> The Forest of the Dead —

KNOWING THE DESTINATION

Retreat — was out of Hope —
Behind — a Sealed Route —
Eternity's White Flag — Before —
And God — at every Gate —

Emily Dickinson (1830-1866),
Our Journey Had Advanced

CHAPTER THREE

RICHARD ROLLE AND *THE CLOUD* AUTHOR

'Faith is inseparable from love.'
Ruth Burrows OCD

More Than Five

The fourteenth century is sometimes referred to as the Golden Age of English Mysticism. This book is an introduction to that Golden Age and the major figures associated with it, especially Walter Hilton of Thurgarton. However, Hilton, Richard Rolle, the anonymous author of *The Cloud of Unknowing,* Julian of Norwich, and Margery Kempe, were not alone. There were other guides to the spiritual life and mystics who experienced unusual visions. This flowering of prayerful mysticism, instruction, and devotion written in the common tongue of the people, was not limited to England as a similar phenomenon was happening on the continent. For example, there was Meister Eckhart in Germany and Saint Catherine of Siena in Italy. England, despite being an island nation, was not isolated from the rest of Europe. Travel between England and the continent was regular. Connections of court, church, and capital formed a complex web of communications between individuals and communities on both sides of the English Channel.

The five individuals described in this volume are the most well-known to us. They were exceptional in certain ways, but in others, they were people of their times. They were part of the energetic movement of vernacular theology of the fourteenth century. This was also a time when the universities, still relatively new institutions, were coming into their own. Theology was shifting away from the chapels of monasteries and into the classrooms of the schools. There was a tension between the rise of scholastic theology with its emphasis on reason and the older monastic theology with its emphasis on the heart.

Richard Rolle: The Mystic of Melody

Richard Rolle died on 29 September 1349, the Feast of St Michael the Archangel. Walter Hilton was nine years old. This was a period of severe outbreak of the plague, which may have taken Rolle's life. He was born around 1300, in the village of Thornton in Yorkshire. Like Hilton, he demonstrated a scholarly aptitude as a boy and later as a young man was admitted to the University of Oxford. His writings demonstrate his intelligence and scholarship. Yet, Rolle dropped out of Oxford before taking a degree. He wanted to pursue a life with God and didn't want to wait until after taking his degree. He didn't pursue ordination, nor did he, as far as we know, approach any church authority to help him discern whether he was called to pursue a spiritual life as a solitary or a monk. Instead, he made his own way into a life of contemplative commitment with the help of his sister. He asked her to meet him in a certain wood with their father's rain hood and two of her tunics.

She agreed willingly and the next day, according to her promise, carried them into the said wood, being quite ignorant what was in her brother's mind. When he received them, he immediately cut off the sleeves and fitted them as best he could for his own purpose. Then he took off his clothes and put on his sister's white tunic next to his skin, and the grey tunic with the sleeves cut out he put over it. He covered his head with the rain hood so that he might present a strange likeness to a hermit. When his sister saw this, she became disturbed and cried, 'My brother is crazy! My brother is crazy!'[25]

62

RICHARD ROLLE AND *THE CLOUD* AUTHOR

Over the centuries many have sympathized with Rolle's sister. The young Rolle, around nineteen years-of-age, wearing his makeshift hermit's habit, runs off into the woods leaving his sister bewildered. If she and other members of the family thought Richard's teenage enthusiasm would wane, they were mistaken. Rolle remained a hermit until his death thirty years later. Despite some initial challenges getting established and accepted as a hermit, Rolle went on to become the most prolific writer of the English mystics and most widely known in the Middle Ages. He eventually situated his hermitage near the Cistercian community of nuns in the village of Hampole in South Yorkshire. Hampole is about an hour north of Thurgarton by car, which would have taken some days to travel in the fourteenth century. There he exercised a ministry of spiritual guidance to women living the contemplative life, including the anchoress, Margaret Kirkby.

Rolle wrote in both Latin and English. It wasn't until later in his ministry that he began to write in Middle English, one of the early pioneers to do so, which enabled him to reach a wider audience of readers. His style and range of works exercised a considerable influence on future writing in English, with one commentator referring to him as 'the true Father of English literature'.[26] Perhaps this comment is too generous and ignores the fact many consider his Latin writings to be more elegant, but regardless, his literary influence was and remains real. He wrote works on the spiritual life, biblical commentaries, and lyrical poetry. Of particular influence was his book, *The Incendium Amoris (The Fire of Love)*. Other works by Rolle include, *Against the Lovers of the World (Contra Amatores Mundi), The Form of Living, The Bee and the Stork, Desire and Delight,* as well as *Emendatio Vitae (Emending of Life)*. In this last work, Rolle employs the metaphor of a ladder with twelve steps to describe the stages of the spiritual life. These are samples of the many titles he wrote. Rolle also translated the biblical book of Psalms into English. The daily recitation of the Psalms was a fundamental practice for those seeking a life of perfection. The psalms form the structure of the monastic day. They also provided a structure of prayer and observance for hermits and anchoresses who, like Rolle, could read.

The Psalms are ancient Hebrew poetry, a collection of prayers, covering a wide range of human emotions and life situations. For example, joy and gratitude as found in Psalm 146:1-2, 'Praise the Lord! Praise the Lord, O my soul! I will praise the Lord as long as I live; I will sing praises to my God all my life long.' Despair and need as found in Psalm 88:1-3, 'O Lord, God of my salvation, at night, when I cry out before you, let my prayer come before you; incline your ear to my cry. For my soul is full of troubles.' Jesus knew the Psalms well and famously quoted Psalm 22 from during his crucifixion, 'My God, My God, why have you forsaken me?' (Matthew 27:26). The Psalms are the Church's original prayer book. Rolle writes concerning their recitation:

> A great fullness of spiritual comfort and joy in God come into the hearts of those who recite or devoutly intone the psalms as an act of praise to Jesus Christ. Indeed, this radiant book is a choice song in God's presence, like a lamp brightening our life, health for the sick heart, honey to a bitter soul. Now see with wholesome instruction it brings agitated and tempestuous souls into a fair and peaceful way of life. The song which gives delight to hearts and instructs the soul has become a sound of singing: with angels whom we cannot hear mingle words of praise.[27]

One evening while he was reciting the Psalms, Rolle had a profound spiritual experience. He tells us:

> I was sitting in a certain chapel and repeating as best I could the night-psalms before I went to supper, I heard about my head it seemed, the joyful ring of psalmody, or perhaps I should say, singing. In my prayer I was reaching out to heaven with heartfelt longing when I became aware, in a way I cannot explain, of a symphony of song, and in myself I sensed a corresponding

harmony at once wholly delectable and heavenly, which persisted in my mind. Then and there my thinking itself turned into melodious song, and my meditation became a poem, and my very prayers and psalms took up the same sound.[28]

Fired Up for God

Rolle explains in his work, *The Fire of Love*, that the contemplative realizing union with God will begin to experience feelings of warmth, the taste of sweetness, as well as the hearing of divine melodies. In one of Rolle's most well-known passages, he describes his first mystical experience of God's burning love. Rolle does so in language that anticipates what John Wesley, the founder of Methodism, reports four centuries later during his conversion experience in 1738, 'my heart was strangely warmed'. Rolle writes:

> I cannot tell you how surprised I was the first time I felt my heart begin to warm. It was a real warmth, too, not imaginary, and it felt as if it were actually on fire. I was astonished at the way the heat surged up, and how this new sensation brought great and unexpected comfort. I had to keep feeling my breast to make sure there was no physical reason for it! But once I realized that it came entirely from within, that this fire of love had no cause, material or sinful, but was the gift of my Maker, I was absolutely delighted and wanted my love to be even greater. Before this infusion of this comfort, I had never thought we exiles could possibly have known such warmth, so sweet was the devotion it kindled. It set my soul aglow as if a real fire was burning there.[29]

Rolle characterizes the spiritual life as a passionate pursuit between God, the lover, and the contemplative, the beloved. He casts the journey to Jerusalem as one with a soundtrack. The song of the Gospel of God's love. The sounds of mystical melody. He compares himself, and all lovers of God, to a nightingale, 'She sings her melody all night long to please him to whom she is united. How much more ought I to sing and as sweetly as I can, to my Jesus Christ, my soul's spouse, through the whole of this present life. Flutelike, I shall pour out melodious, fervent devotion, raising from the heart songs of praise to God.'[30] This lyrical devotion, described in the human experience of romantic love, and the courtly love traditions of Europe, is characteristic of the tradition of Christian mysticism. This lyrical emphasis is often found in the Bible's most erotic and sensuous book, *The Song of Songs.* A book that celebrates physical beauty and the passion of lovers, 'Let him kiss me with the kisses of his mouth! For your love is better than wine' (Song of Songs 1:2).

For centuries, this Old Testament book has been a source of Christian reflection by mystics and teachers of prayer. They have used the language of this book to hint at the kind of intimacy that can be known between the soul and God. Contemplative experience of the infinite challenges our finite human abilities to understand or describe. For Rolle, the pilgrimage to Jerusalem is a cosmic love story. It is a journey of longing love, joyful anticipation, and, when granted by God, profound union. After Rolle's death, there was a movement, never successful, to secure his official canonization as a saint by the medieval church.

ॐ

I first went to Hampole after being warmly welcomed at nearby St Laurence Church. They have a memorial display dedicated to Richard Rolle. In past years they held an annual Rolle festival. It is believed that the hermit visited the church during his time in the region. The church has been a place of Christian worship for more than 1000 years. Outside of the church building, in the cemetery yard, is a medieval stone cross. These stone crosses, which can still be found across the country, were focal points for devotion and preaching in the Middle Ages. I was tempted to deliver a sermon when I saw the stone cross, but I had mercy on my hosts and got in my car and made my way to Hampole.

RICHARD ROLLE AND *THE CLOUD* AUTHOR

Hampole is still a small village. There are no remains of the medieval church, nunnery, or Rolle's hermitage. Behind the modern village buildings are green fields that stretch out along a simple road that leads to the motorway. There is a small memorial to Rolle near the bus stop. Some of the stones in the current farm buildings are probably from the ruins of the original medieval convent Rolle would have known. It is a peaceful place, serene, quiet, and tucked between the hustle of the motorway and the activity of the village. Not a bad location for a hermit, even more than six hundred years later. As I looked across the fields, the sun warming my face, it was not hard for me to imagine the hermit sitting in his chapel, reaching out to God. Here is one of Rolle's prayers from *The Fire of Love*.

Come, my Saviour, comfort my soul!
Make me steadfast in my love for you,
So that I never cease loving.
Take the grief from me when it is my time to die,
For there is no sinner who cannot rejoice
Once he be perfectly converted to you.
Remember your compassion, Jesus most sweet,
that my life may shine resplendent in your power;
and so that I can overcome my enemy
bestow on me your mighty salvation!
I ask all this of you lest I be lost with the son of perdition.
Since my mind has been fire with holy love,
I am filled with longing to see your Majesty.
Therefore I endure poverty,
I despise earthly dignity,
And I care for no sort of honour.
Your friendship is my glory.
When I began to love, your love laid hold of my heart,
and would allow me to desire nothing save love.
There is delightful warmth in the loving heart,
which has consumed gloom and trouble in its fiery
burning love.

And from it has issued sweetness,
And in particular, music which comes in to soothe the soul,
for there you, my God and my comfort,
have set up your Temple.[31]

Mystic to Mystic: Rolle and Hilton

Richard Rolle believed the solitary life was the superior form of
Christian life. In his view, it afforded the serious Christian the most
freedom to pursue contemplation, even more than a monk or nun
within a monastery. Rolle's writings were already influential when
Walter Hilton came of age. Hilton is familiar with some of Rolle's
writings and may have been inspired by him to pursue the solitary
life. However, Hilton quit being a hermit and joined the monastic
community of Augustinian Canons in Thurgarton. Hilton, more
than any of the other mystics in this volume, affirms the validity
of all three states of life: the active, the contemplative, and the
mixed. Rolle did not believe it was possible to mix the active and
contemplative lives. If he had been in Hilton's place in responding
to the worldly lord's question about what he should do with his life,
Rolle may have advised him to leave his family and become a hermit.
The larger disagreement between Hilton and Rolle, at least as most
scholars have interpreted it, is over extraordinary phenomena.

In *The Scale of Perfection*, Hilton writes to his anchoress reader:
Understand that visions or revelations of any kind of spirit,
appearing in the body or in the imagination, asleep or awake, or
any other feeling in the bodily senses made in spiritual fashion –
either in sound by the ear, or tasting in the mouth, or smelling
to the nose, or else any heat that can be felt like fire glowing and
warming the breast or any other part of the body, or anything
that can be felt by bodily sense, however comforting and
pleasing it may be – these are not true contemplation. They are
only simple and secondary – though they are good – compared
with virtues and the knowledge and love of God.[32]

For Hilton, extraordinary spiritual phenomena are secondary and not to be sought after. The primary focus of the spiritual life, including the contemplative life, is growth in love for God and neighbour. Aligned with these goals is personal growth in character and virtue, not in esoteric abilities or experiences.

Nonetheless, Rolle and Hilton are both committed to seeking the Triune God through the person of Jesus Christ. Both spiritual writers emphasize the importance of humility and love, in serving one's neighbour in the active life and in seeking union with God in the contemplative life. Both writers use the imagery of fire, a rich metaphor long used by Christian mystics and spiritual teachers. Rolle's powerful and unusual experiences, whatever their merits or limitations, remind us that it is possible we will experience strange and wonderful things along the road to Jerusalem. When such phenomena distract us from the way, they are to be left behind on the side of the road. In so much as they help us make progress on the way, they can be encouragements for ourselves and others. These kinds of phenomena at their best give us glimpses of the wonder of God and all created things, which we often perceive in this life, to quote St Paul, only 'through a mirror darkly' (1 Corinthians 13:12).

The Cloud *author: The Mystic of Unknowing*

If we know less than we'd like to about Walter Hilton and Richard Rolle, we know even less about the life of the author of *The Cloud*. The dialect of Middle English in the surviving manuscripts we have seems to indicate that he was, like Hilton, from the East Midlands. Most scholars believe he was a monk, probably a Carthusian. The Carthusians were founded in the eleventh century by St Bruno. They are an enclosed contemplative order, dedicated to a combination of community life and solitude. *The Cloud* author wrote several works on the spiritual life such as *Letter on Prayer, Discernment of Stirrings, The Book of Privy Council,* and most famously, *The Cloud of Unknowing.*

Some scholars speculate that the book was written in Beauvale Priory, a Carthusian House, in the East Midlands, about a day's walk from Thurgarton. Hilton's Cambridge classmate and friend, Adam Horsley, entered the Carthusian Order at Beauvale. This could help explain the familiarity that *The Cloud* author seems to have with Hilton's *Scale of Perfection.* Not that Horsley was necessarily our unknown author, but that he could have shared Hilton's writings with our unknown author. As with many details of the lives and manuscripts of the English mystics, we cannot be certain. This book is written by an older monk to a younger monk. For ease of reference, we will refer to the author of *The Cloud* as Ignotus, which is the Latin word for unknown.[33] Ignotus provides instruction about pursuing a particular form of prayer. An advanced form of preparation for contemplation that is not for beginners. Ignotus's warning to his protégé about the kind of people who should and should not read his book has amused and sobered readers over the centuries:

To you, whoever you are, who may have this book in your possession, whether as owner or custodian, conveyor or borrower: I lay this charge upon you and implore you with all the power and force that the bond of charity can command. You are not to read it yourself or to others, or to copy it; nor are you to allow it so to be read in private or in public or copied willingly and deliberately, insofar as this is possible, except by someone or to someone who, as far as you know, has resolved with steadfast determination, truly and sincerely to be a perfect follower of Christ; and this not only in the active life, but in the contemplative life, at the highest point which a perfect soul in this present life can possibly reach, with the help of grace, whilst it still dwells in this mortal body.[34]

A legitimate question for any reader, medieval or modern, is who can read this book? Even if we grant that Ignotus is using hyperbole, it seems that his work is intended for a very small group of people, vowed contemplatives, monks, or solitaries, who have progressed beyond the basics of the active and contemplative lives. In other words, those who are making good progress on their pilgrimage to Jerusalem. How the earliest recipients of this book responded to this warning is unknown. Today, *The Cloud of Unknowing* is one of the most popular English mystical works, read by people who come from a variety of religious and spiritual backgrounds. It is a foundational text for the twentieth-century centring prayer movement started by the three American Trappist monks, Thomas Meninger, Thomas Keating, and Basil Pennington. Most modern readers do not fit the description Ignotus had in mind when he wrote the book. However, some modern readers do fit the additional descriptions of people who should *not* read the book: 'As for the worldly chatterboxes, who brazenly flatter or censure themselves or others, the rumour-mongers, the gossips, the tittle-tattlers and the fault-finders of every sort, I would not want them ever to see my book.'[35]

After these warnings, Ignotus's tone is warm and encouraging. He demonstrates insight into the states of prayer and human psychology. His role is that of a spiritual guide and director. Ignotus urges the younger monk, 'Lift up your heart to God with a humble impulse of love; and have Godself as your aim, not any of God's goods.'[36] The lover of God, a frequent description for a mystic, is someone who wants to be with God, to experience God in the depths of their being, and who has no ulterior motive in seeking God. Often in my prayer, I have ulterior motives in seeking God. I want to pray for a particular person and for a specific world situation. I want strength for a difficult day and forgiveness for my sin. Ignotus is not saying there isn't a time for these sorts of prayers. There is, but not during this kind of prayer.

This kind of prayer reminds me of an old story about a medieval peasant woman who used to sit in the back of an empty church for hours at a time. Someone asked her, 'What are you doing back there?' She replied, 'I look at him. He looks at me.' This is suggestive of the kind of prayer Ignotus is teaching in *The Cloud of Unknowing*. The purpose of this prayer is to be with God and to open oneself up to the possibility of God's power, presence, and love. Prayer, in whatever form, does not force God to show up. Christian prayer, in general, and the English Mystical Tradition in particular, is always invitational. It's a way of opening the door of one's heart and saying, 'God, I'd love for you to come in. I'll be waiting expectedly. Whatever you decide, whatever happens, I will strive to love you more and to be thankful.'

In fact, Ignotus wants us to go beyond this simple kind of imaginative prayer. He wants us to go beyond the use of words, familiar understandings, and images of God so we can only have what he calls 'a naked intent'. The idea is to embrace as much as we can for the duration of this kind of prayer—a simple posture of receptivity. We are to have a posture devoid of language and even thought, but full of love. Its goal is a silent form of prayer—a silent mind, a silent voice, and a still body. This is an internal stillness and silence that opens the heart to the mystery of God. It is the personal application of Psalm 46:10, 'Be still and know that I am God.' Ignotus, while wanting to minimize imagery, cannot help but use some imagery to describe his method of prayer. His chief images are the cloud of forgetting, the cloud of unknowing, and the dart of love. Ignotus writes, 'Come to this cloud, and live and work in it as I bid you. Just as this cloud of unknowing is above you, between you and your God, in the same way, you must put beneath you a cloud of forgetting, between you and all the creatures that have ever been made.'[37] For Ignotus, no matter how far the contemplative advances in this life, God is hidden and mediated through a cloud of unknowing. The limited human can never fully comprehend the infinite God. He also writes, 'For one thing I must tell you. There never yet existed nor ever shall, so pure a creature so high in contemplation who did not find this high and wonderful cloud of unknowing between him and his God.'[38] The contemplative must strive to unknow their intellectual and imaginative understandings of God for the duration of this particular kind of prayer.

Clear Your Thoughts, Open Your Heart

This exercise is a clearing of all thought. It is a setting aside of regular God consciousness through ordinary human cognition and perception to experience a deeper God consciousness. An encounter with God, according to Ignotus, can only be experienced through love. The contemplative sits figuratively between these two clouds, tossing all their thoughts into the cloud of forgetting, while striving to pierce the cloud of unknowing with a dart of longing love. Ignotus writes, 'If then, you are determined to stand and not to fall, never cease from your endeavour, but constantly beat with a sharp dart of longing love upon this cloud of unknowing which is between you and your God. Avoid thinking of anything under God and do not leave this exercise no matter what happens.'[39] Some translations use a sword, shaft, or arrow to describe the piercing of the cloud of unknowing.[40] It can also be conceived of as a knocking. Ignotus refers to the contemplative who offers, 'a humble impulse of love to God, knocking secretly on the cloud of unknowing between him and his God.'[41] Without this central love dimension, one might unfairly characterize *The Cloud's* teaching as simply a method of clearing the mind. This is not a method of meditation in the sense of clearing the mind for mental, emotional, or spiritual benefit. It is a method of prayer for deepening a relationship with God by cultivating an interior receptivity to God.

The contemplative cannot be certain they will receive a palatable gift of the experience of divine love. However, they can be assured that God is gracious and willing to give this gift to those who seek it. Those who like Mary of Bethany, sitting at the feet of Jesus, position themselves to receive it. This experience of love is not exclusive to feelings. This experience can include and surpass feelings, sustained only by the will to love. It is the choice to love God. It is the choice to wait on God as an act of love, and to keep at it even if nothing remarkable happens. Ignotus advises, 'So, follow humbly this simple stirring of love in your heart; I do not mean in your physical heart, but in your spiritual heart, which is your will.'[42] Modern practitioners of centring prayer and other similar forms of silent prayer suggest practicing this method daily for a set time, perhaps twenty minutes to an hour.

Ignotus is well acquainted with the formidable challenge of clearing the mind that this kind of prayer presents. Distractions, temptations, and otherwise good thoughts threaten to derail the contemplative's attention to God alone. This is why he insists that those who try this kind of prayer do so only after making good progress in the spiritual life. The traditional monastic program of growing in virtue, fighting vice, and overcoming sin provides a level of spiritual fitness that makes it possible for the contemplative to engage in this higher kind of prayer. While God can grant this sort of experience to whoever God wishes, it is ordinarily given to those who have by grace and effort prepared themselves to receive it.

For such individuals, like his younger counterpart, Ignotus suggests the use of an anchor word to deal with distractions. An anchor word is 'of one syllable rather than of two, for the shorter is the better with this exercise of the spirit. Such a one is the word, "God" or the word, "love".'[43] Its purpose is to deflect, push away, and protect the contemplative from resuming ordinary human consciousness; that is, from thinking about something. When distraction comes, the anchor word is invoked – 'This word is to be your shield'.[44] The word is not to be thought about or given any consideration. The anchor word's purpose is to re-centre the contemplative to a minimally self-consciousness posture of receptivity. Ignotus says, 'With this word you are to strike down every kind of thought under the cloud of forgetting; so that if any thought should press upon you and ask you what you would have, answer it with no other word but this one.'[45]

Ignotus warns his readers that engaging in this practice will be difficult. While labour-intensive, even as guided and sustained by God's grace, the fruits of the exercise can be liberating. Ignotus describes the contemplative experience of God as follows, 'Whenever you are aware that your mind is occupied with no created thing, whether material or spiritual, but only with the substance of God himself, as indeed the mind is and can be in the experience of the exercise described in this book, then you are above yourself and under your God.'[46] This experience of high contemplation, of deep prayer, is largely ineffable. Ignotus writes that this experience is:

> Something which you are at a loss to describe, which moves you to describe you know not what. You must not care if you understand no more of it; just press on with the exercise more and more, so that you are always engaged in it. To put it more clearly, let it do with you and lead you as it will. Let it be the one that works; you simply must consent to it. Simply look at it, and just let it be. Do not interfere with it, as though you wished to help it on, lest you spill it all.[47]

Ignotus' method is for cultivating contemplative consciousness. This requires the ability to set aside ordinary consciousness for the barest of self-awareness. He describes this as 'a simple knowing and feeling of your own being'.[48] Ignotus acknowledges that a total loss of self-awareness seldom happens. When it does, it's a matter of God's gift and a practised human receptivity. 'Without a very special grace which God gives out of his absolute bounty and along with it a corresponding capacity on your part of receiving this grace, this simple awareness and experience of your being can in no way be destroyed.'[49] St Paul writes, 'God's love is poured into our hearts through the Holy Spirit that has been given to us' (Romans 5:5). Developing a greater awareness and receiving a greater measure of this love are the two-fold purposes of this kind of prayer. Most Christians will only experience this kind of God awareness intermittently and occasionally. Ignotus's method of prayer is a witness to the deeper, interior journey of the heart. A method he says is only for some and even then, only under the direction of an experienced guide. For Ignotus, the pilgrimage to Jerusalem is a pilgrimage within the deepest depths of the ocean of prayer. A pilgrimage of longing love that seeks to penetrate the mystery of God. He writes, 'For the high road and the shortest road thither to heaven and contemplation is measured by desire and not by yards.'[50]

Mystic to Mystic: Ignotus and Hilton

In the past, there were some scholars who thought that Hilton was the unknown author of *The Cloud of Unknowing*. This has been summarily disproven. The two authors have different purposes in their major works, *The Scale of Perfection* and *The Cloud of Unknowing*. Hilton provides instruction concerning the major stages and practices of the spiritual life. Ignotus teaches about one aspect of that life, deep prayer and high contemplation. Ignotus assumes his readers have already made progress in many of the teachings Hilton writes about.

In *The Cloud* he writes, 'There are certain preparatory exercises which should occupy the attention of the contemplative apprentice: the lesson, the meditation, and the petition. You will find a much better treatment of these three than I can manage in the book of another author. So, I need not rehearse their qualities here.'[51] Here Ignotus is probably referring to the influential work I mentioned in a past chapter, Guigo II's *Ladder of Monks*. Some believe Ignotus is referring to Hilton's *Scale of Perfection*. Regardless, both Hilton and Ignotus draw from this common spiritual heritage, and both assume the spiritual life is developmental. While each person is unique, there are typical patterns of progress and difficulty faced by most on the way to Jerusalem. Both writers acknowledge that God can operate outside of these usual patterns.

In addition, both writers stress humility as a foundation for pursuing a serious spiritual life. This is non-negotiable, especially for those seeking contemplative experience. Both recognize that humility is not something one has or doesn't have, but as with all the virtues, there are tried and true ways of growing in humility. For the English mystics, these ways are not a self-help guided process, but a Spirit-help guided process. The growth requires our effort but is made possible by God's grace and, over time, is quickened and enabled by God. For long years, *The Cloud of Unknowing* has been a revelation to many people who sensed, or at least hoped, there was more to prayer and more to God than petitions and praises. In *The Cloud,* they have discovered a new dimension of prayer that silently sinks into the dark depths of God.

Mystic to Mystic: Rolle and Ignotus

Richard Rolle's major work, *The Fire of Love,* is characterized by a form of cataphatic spirituality. Cataphatic comes from the Greek word *kataphasis*, meaning affirmation. Cataphatic approaches to God are positive and affirmative. They say that God is like something. God is like the very best human father one could imagine. Who God is and what God is like is expressed through what we know from the created order. Ignotus's major work, *The Cloud of Unknowing,* is characterized by a form of apophatic spirituality. Apophatic comes from the Greek word *apophemi*, meaning to deny. God as God is not like a human father, God is not human, God is not finite, and so on. All our affirmations and positive ways of speaking about God have their limitations. This is why for theology and spirituality to be robust and honest, the *via positiva*, as it is called in Latin, what we can affirm about God, must be balanced by the *via negativa*, what we can say is not true about God.

Cataphatic spirituality encounters God through the five senses, through creation, art, music, poetry, and ritual. These are the primary ways most people encounter God and practise their faith. It is a spirituality of knowing. Apophatic spirituality finds God through negation, by pulling away the layers of human analogy and created things to a deep inner awareness of God's presence. In apophatic theology, God is understood by defining what God is not. It is a spirituality of unknowing. Apophatic spirituality reminds us that God is infinite and we are finite. Our descriptions of God are in a certain sense, even the most sophisticated, the very best of poetry. Poetry carries the remarkable power to convey what technical language cannot. Theology in this sense hints at, evokes, and approximately (though not precisely), describes God and the things of God. A God who could be measured precisely, whether in meters or yards, would not be God at all. This doesn't diminish the role of language or the value of precise theological formulations. Technical language, leaning on reason and logic, and poetic language, leaning on imagination and intuition, are both essential in the work of theology. The limitations of language require us to handle all language about God with the greatest care. Freeing us from a paralysis of analysis in this regard is the Christian claim that God desires to be known. God is revealed in Scripture and most fully in Jesus Christ. The work of the Holy Spirit in the Church and world reveals God. God works through our imperfect language and with our limited capabilities. 'No one has ever seen God. It is God the only Son, who is close to the Father's heart, who has made him known' (John 1:18). This is good news.

Rolle and Ignotus cannot fully describe their mystical experiences. This is the limitation of all human language, whether expressed positively or negatively. Part of the journey to Jerusalem is learning a new language, a language of the Spirit. A language of lived theology, poetry, and spirituality that corresponds however imperfectly to the sights, sounds, and setbacks of the spiritual life. The writings of all the Christian mystics, including those in the English Mystical Tradition, contain time-tested ways of speaking about God and the ways to God. Each mystic has their own way of speaking. To understand them fully, you must spend time with them, reading their works, talking to their friends, and seeking the God they are seeking. Schools of mystics, like those in this book, unite in a common dialect of faith and spirituality. As we immerse ourselves in their teachings and make our own way along God's highway, we will learn to speak a version of their language. The English mystics' experiences of God and their ways of speaking about them will enrich and expand our existing dialects of the divine. Dialects we've learned from our families, cultures, and religious traditions. Eventually, we will develop our own way of speaking about God, with our own distinct voice, even as we speak in ways that others can understand.

NEXT STEPS

- Read *The Fire of Love* by Richard Rolle
- Read *The Cloud of Unknowing* by Ignotus
- Find companions for your journey to Jerusalem
- Learn about one or more of these topics on your own:
  Vernacular Theology   Cistercians   The Song of Songs
  Apophatic   Centring Prayer   Consciousness   Cataphatic

PRAY

> I ask you, Lord Jesus,
> to develop in me, your lover,
> an immeasurable urge towards you,
> an affection that is unbounded,
> a longing that is unrestrained,
> a fervour that throws discretion to the winds!
> The more worthwhile our love for you,
> all the more pressing does it become.
> Reason cannot hold it in check,
> fear does not make it tremble,
> wise judgment does not temper it.
>
> Richard Rolle, Chapter 17, *The Fire of Love*

A PILGRIMAGE OF THE HEART

EXERCISES

Choose one or more exercises to enrich and deepen your learning from this chapter.

- *Ponder a Psalm*

  Read slowly and silently through either Psalm 23 or Psalm 121. Take your time. Let the words sink into your mind and heart. Then read the Psalm aloud. If so moved, pray in response to the Psalm. If not so moved, take note of what comforts you and challenges you about the psalm.

- *Clear Your Mind*

  Ignotus's exercise is not simply a clearing of the mind. It is a specific kind of prayer, a spiritual exercise, to be engaged in after significant preparation. Nonetheless, part of the technique of this kind of prayer requires an ability to clear all thoughts from the active mind. Sit down in a quiet place and attempt to think of nothing for one minute. Try two if you are brave. Take note of why this was an easy or difficult exercise for you.

QUESTIONS

1. What were your thoughts and feelings when reading about how Richard Rolle dropped out of university and then ran off into the woods wearing a makeshift hermit's outfit? Can you imagine someone doing something like that today?

2. What is your experience with the book of Psalms from the Old Testament? Do you have any favourite psalms? Why do you think the prayerful recitation of the psalms, which cover a range of human emotions and situations, have been an integral part of the practice of Christian spirituality for centuries?

3. Richard Rolle experienced mystical sensations of warmth, sweetness, and song. These experiences were not unknown in the Middle Ages, but Rolle emphasized them as key signs of spiritual maturity and growth. Have you ever had experiences like these? Would you want to? Is the point of Christian

mysticism to experience unusual phenomena like these?

4. What do you think of Ignotus' warning at the start of *The Cloud of Unknowing?* Do you think there are certain spiritual practices or disciplines people should wait to practise until they are more experienced in the spiritual life? What harm, if any, could happen to someone ignoring Ignotus's warning and as a beginner trying his method of prayer?

5. Have you ever thought of the problem of language and faith? The challenge of finite human beings using imperfect human language to describe an infinite God? Why does the author say that both positive and negative approaches to God are needed in theology and spirituality? What are the technical names for these approaches?

SIDE TRIP

Batter my heart, three-person'd God, for you
As yet but knock, breathe, shine, and seek to mend;
That I may rise and stand, o'erthrow me, and bend
Your force to break, blow, burn, and make me new.
I, like an usurp'd town to another due,
Labor to admit you, but oh, to no end;
Reason, your viceroy in me, me should defend,
But is captiv'd, and proves weak or untrue.
Yet dearly I love you, and would be lov'd fain,
But am betroth'd unto your enemy;
Divorce me, untie or break that knot again,
Take me to you, imprison me, for I,
Except you enthrall me, never shall be free,
Nor ever chaste, except you ravish me.

John Donne (1572-1631),
Batter my heart, three-person'd God

CHAPTER FOUR

JULIAN OF NORWICH AND MARGERY KEMPE

'Humbly I adore thee, Verity unseen.'
St Thomas Aquinas

Women Who Speak in Church

The female mystics of the fourteenth century are a paradox. They embody and challenge the oft-quoted phrase, variously attributed, that 'well behaved women seldom make history'. By their behaving well as lovers of God they made history. In their behaving well as lovers of God, they sometimes behaved in ways thought inappropriate by others, especially men in positions of ecclesiastical and secular authority.

Any medieval woman who dared to admit to mystical experience risked her reputation and possibly her life. However, contemplative life as a nun or anchoress was socially acceptable for women. Contemplative nuns lived in cloistered monasteries. Anchoresses were sealed inside of four walls. Neither kind of contemplative ordinarily taught doctrine, preached, gave spiritual commentary on contemporary events, or wrote works of theology. These activities were mostly considered inappropriate for women and for most men.

Yet, mysticism in the Middle Ages, especially the later Middle Ages, became a socially acceptable, if sometimes controversial way, for women to exercise public influence in affairs of church, state, and society. Neither Julian of Norwich nor Margery Kempe exercised the kind of public ministry that their continental counterparts, such as St Bridget of Sweden and St Catherine of Siena did in the same century. The influence of each English mystic, while somewhat significant in their own lifetimes, simmered over the centuries in more or less obscurity until the twentieth century.

Julian of Norwich: The Mothering Mystic

Julian of Norwich was born around 1342, only two years after Hilton's birth in 1340. They were almost exact contemporaries. It is likely Julian lived all her life in Norwich, within the historic county of Norfolk. Like Hilton, she would have been a child during some of the worst outbreaks of the plague. We don't know anything concrete about Julian until she is thirty years old. Even the name we know her by is probably taken from St Julian's Church where she later became an anchoress. In her writings, she tells us she became seriously ill. We don't know what kind of illness she had. Different scholars and writers have speculated that she had been a mother and wife who had lost her family during the plague and others that she had been a nun. We cannot be certain. Despite her claim to be unlettered, her writings demonstrate considerable theological learning. Most of what we know about her comes from what she tells us through the accounts of her mystical experiences. Bishop Rowan Williams, the 104th Archbishop of Canterbury, has said that her writings 'may well be the most important work of Christian reflection in the English language'.

On 13 May 1373, Julian is on her deathbed. Her mother is present. She writes, 'My priest was sent for to be present at my end, and by the time he came my eyes were fixed and I could not speak. He set the cross before my face and said, "I have brought you the image of your maker and Saviour. Look at and take comfort from it".'[52] As Julian observed the crucifix, the first of her sixteen showings began. The showings or visions continued in succession, with the final vision happening the day after. Julian experiences a complete recovery of health in conjunction with the showings. She writes down the visions in what is now called the 'Short Text', shortly thereafter. After some twenty years of reflection, she writes another work, called the 'Long Text.' The long text is usually the text people refer to when talking about Julian. The book's title is *The Revelations of Divine Love.* Hers is the first book known to be written by a woman in English. Sometime after her recovery, she became an anchoress. An anchorite or anchoress was a form of the solitary life. Unlike hermits, like Richard Rolle, who could travel from location to location, an anchoress was limited to one location. Her location was the cell attached to St Julian's Church, Norwich. Norwich was the second-largest city in England at the time. It was a major centre commercially, politically, and religiously. Like other medieval cities, it endured outbreaks of plague and violence.

An anchoress had to get support from the local bishop before entering her cell or anchorhold. She had to demonstrate aptitude for a contemplative life as well as account for how she would be supported financially. Julian had a lay assistant who helped attend to her basic needs, such as bringing her food. From records, it appears that she had two helpers over the years, the first Alice, and the second, Sarah. Before entering the anchorhold, which would be sealed off, the funeral service was prayed. The anchoress in effect 'died to the world'. [53] It was a dramatic entry into a life of seclusion. A life committed to contemplation and a literal closing of the door to pray, echoing Jesus' words from the Sermon on the Mount: 'But whenever you pray, go into your room and shut the door and pray to your Father who is in secret; and your Father who sees in secret will reward you' (Matthew 6:6). We have records of some of Julian's financial supporters, such as Isabell Ufford, Countess of Suffolk, and John Plumpton, a citizen of Norwich, leaving her gifts of support in their wills. She lived a long life by medieval standards, dying sometime after 1416. The life of an anchoress followed a particular contemplative pattern. In addition to the writings of anchoresses like Julian and the guidance given to them by writers like Walter Hilton, our main source of information about the life of anchoresses is the thirteenth-century book, *Ancrene Wisse* or *Guide for Anchoresses*. This guide includes the provision, 'My dear sisters, you must not have any animal except a cat.' Since an anchoress was to be primarily occupied with her prayers and her life confined with her cell, any other animal would presumably distract her from her vocation. A cat, being independent, could come and go and largely look after itself. This historical detail lends credence to the innumerable artistic depictions of Julian with a cat.

The physical enclosure of the anchorhold was intended to facilitate the inward journey of the anchoress toward God. Julian's cell, a monastic term for a room, was attached to St Julian's Church. She had one window that allowed her to look into the church and participate in the Mass and receive Holy Communion. She had another window to the world where she was available to give spiritual counsel. This open-window policy meant that anchoresses, unlike cloistered contemplative nuns, could have a form of ministry to the world. We know that Julian had a reputation in her lifetime as a wise spiritual guide. In fact, as far as we know, this was her only reputation in her lifetime. It appears her visions were not widely known. It's probable that she trusted only a few, perhaps her confessor and lay assistants, with knowledge of her experiences. It wasn't until the twentieth century that her writings became widely known.

ᥱᢒ

The sun was bright and warm in Norwich. Remarkably, it had been this way for a few days. It was one of the last days of the summer. The streets were full of people of all ages and different backgrounds—parents with their young children and couples walking hand-in-hand. There were young people walking about in energetic small groups. The sights and sounds of traffic, cars, taxis, and buses, added to the hustle and bustle of the city's landscape. For the moment, I was shielded from this human activity. I was sitting in silence facilitated by the stone walls of St Julian's Church. I'd been praying in Julian's cell. There is a discernible sense of the holy in that simple space—a pew, a candle, and a plain altar with a crucifix above it on the wall. I was there on a pilgrimage, and it was a remarkable feeling. Julian was one of the first Christian mystics I read. She helped me to embrace Christianity seriously. Her writings encouraged me to seek the road to Jerusalem before I knew what the road to Jerusalem was about. After praying, I left the church to walk back, past the Julian Centre, up to All Hallows Guest House, where I was staying.

Every year pilgrims come to Norwich from around the world to visit Julian's cell. Some participate in events held at the Julian Centre and some stay at the All Hallow's Guesthouse, which is a former convent. I was wearing the habit of my order that day, a set of black and white robes. Before I got back to the guest house where I was staying, a man stopped me. He looked like he was on his way to work, dressed in a pressed shirt and trousers. He asked me what the bowl of hazelnuts was about in the church. The church is open for prayer and reflection every day. The man had previously been in Julian's cell and had noticed the bowl of hazelnuts displayed there. His question led us into a friendly street-side conversation about mysticism, eastern forms of spirituality, and Julian. After our chat, I carried on to my room at All Hallows and he went to his job. The pilgrimage of life, especially once you decide to seek Jerusalem, is often like that. You meet people along the way that bless you with their questions and presence and, hopefully, in turn, you bless them with your questions and presence. People you could never have imagined meeting before beginning your pilgrimage. One of Julian's most famous showings concerns a hazelnut:

And in this vision he also showed me a little thing, the size of a hazelnut, lying in the palm of my hand and it was round as a ball, as it seemed to me. I looked at it and thought, 'What can this be?' And the answer came to me in a general way, like this, 'It is all that is made.' I wondered how it could last, for it seemed to me so small that it might have disintegrated suddenly into nothingness. And I was answered in my understanding, 'It lasts, and always will, because God loves it; and in the same way everything has its being through the love of God.'[54]

The hazelnut is a reassuring image of God's sustaining power and love for all things. The hazelnut is small, perhaps even insignificant, yet it is given grand significance by being cared for by God. This vision Julian received during a time of terrible suffering and plague is evocative of the Christian emphasis on hope—hope in the worst of circumstances and hope in a hopeful God. This is the hope that we are held, enfolded, and enclosed by God. Julian writes, 'God is our clothing that out of love enwraps us and enfolds us, embraces us and wholly encloses us, surrounding us for tender love, so that God can never leave us.'[55] Julian's vision has a resonance with an African American spiritual, a song entitled, 'He's Got the Whole World in His Hands.' The six stanzas repeat a single line three times, before returning to the refrain of 'He's got the whole world in his hands.'

> He's got the whole world in his hands.
> He's got the wind and the rain in his hands.
> He's got the tiny little baby in his hands.
> He's got you and me, brother, in his hands,
> He's got you and me, sister, in his hands
> He's got everybody here in his hands.

If we were to add a stanza by Julian it might go:

He's got the tiny little hazelnut in his hands.
He's got the tiny little hazelnut in his hands.
He's got the tiny little hazelnut in his hands.
He's got the whole world in His hands.

Considering the rest of Julian's revelations, we could just as easily title that song, 'She's Got the Whole World in Her Hands'. In response to one of her other showings, Julian writes, 'And so I saw that God rejoices that he is our father and God rejoices that he is our mother.'[56] A few pages later she adds, 'The mother's service is closest, most willing, and most sure; closest because it is most natural, most willing because it is most loving, and most sure because it is most true.'[57] Julian's revelations and reflections on them develop a remarkable theology of God around the idea of motherhood. There is also the motherhood of the Church. God enjoins Julian and all who read her showings to 'hold fast to the faith of Holy Church and find there our dearest mother in the communion of saints; for a single individual may often feel broken, but the whole body of Holy Church was never broken nor ever shall be, without end. And therefore, it is a safe thing—good and gracious—to wish humbly and strongly to be sustained by and united to our mother, Holy Church.'[58]

For Julian, the pilgrimage to Jerusalem is made as part of the mystic fellowship of the Church. This fellowship of pilgrims supports her life as she does theirs. Julian lives physically and spiritually within the heart of the Church. However much her life is hidden from others, sealed off from the world, all that she does is a participation in the Body of Christ, the Church. Chief among these pilgrims, the whole body of Christians past, present, and future, is Mary, the mother of Jesus. 'Our Lady is our mother, in whom we are enclosed and born of her in Christ; for she who is mother of our Saviour is mother of all who will be saved in our Saviour.'[59] The motherhoods of the Church and Mary are intimately tied with Christ, since Jesus was born of her body and the Church is the body of Christ.

A PILGRIMAGE OF THE HEART

Past spiritual writers like St Anselm, Archbishop of Canterbury in the twelfth century, have written about the motherhood of Christ, but Julian develops this idea more robustly and creatively than all before her. She urges her readers to flee to God, to flee to Christ like a child does to its mother: 'But Christ wants us to behave like a child; for when it is upset or frightened it runs quickly to its mother for help as fast as it can; so, Christ wants us to behave, saying, "My kind mother, my gracious mother, my dearest mother, take pity on me".'[60] Julian compares Jesus' Passion to a form of giving birth. His suffering on the cross is likened to the labour pains of pregnancy through which all are born spiritually:

> We know that our mothers bear us and bring us into this world to suffering and death, and yet our true mother, Jesus, he, all love, gives birth to us into joy and to endless life — blessed may he be! So, he sustains us with himself in love and was in labour for the full time, he who wanted to suffer the sharpest pangs and the most grievous sufferings that ever were or ever shall be, and at the last he died. And when he had finished and so given birth to us in bliss, not even all this could satisfy his marvellous love.[61]

The mother is willing to suffer the pains of childbirth to birth a new life into the world. In an analogous way, God in Christ is willing to suffer the cross to birth new life, for us, and the whole world.

Julian's hope is akin to a beaming light in the darkest and most dangerous of valleys. Julian wrestles with the suffering and sin of the world. She humbly challenges God to help her make sense of the vast chasm she perceives between God's goodness and the world's brokenness. She is intimately familiar with suffering through her experience of illness and of divine love through her experience of God. She is assured that God is with her and God is with all on the pilgrim path. She writes, 'I saw God in a point: And he showed himself on earth in another way, as if on pilgrimage: that is to say, he is here with us, leading us, and will be until he has brought us all up to his bliss in heaven.'[62] Julian's experience of contemplation, of the presence of God, reassures her to trust and to have faith even in the face of the worst that life has to offer. Like Julian, we are all invited to make our way to Jerusalem with a posture of hope, born of the experience of God's mothering care. To trust in God's assurance, God gives Julian a phrase, a phrase repeated throughout her revelations. The phrase is, 'All shall be well'. These four words have now taken on a life of their own, being repeated by people all over the world. This phrase is found in slight variations throughout her book, such as when Julian tells us, 'And so our good Lord answered all the questions and doubts that I could raise, saying most comfortingly, "I may make all things well; I can make all things well, and I will make all things well, and I shall make all things well; and you will see for yourself that all manner of things shall be well".'[63]

Mystic to Mystic: Julian and Walter

Julian demonstrates familiarity with many aspects of the traditional spiritual life taught by Hilton and others in her *Revelations of Divine Love*. Yet, her primary purpose is not to teach a particular ascetical or mystical system for approaching God, rather it is to share the wonderful revelations of God's intimate, gracious, forgiving, and sustaining love. Along the way, Julian provides instruction and abundant insight into the spiritual life and the way to Jerusalem. Hilton's *Scale of Perfection* is written for an anchoress. Written to instruct and encourage her in her contemplative vocation. Julian is familiar with some of Hilton's ideas and may have had access to *The Scale*. Both writers emphasize the dignity of human beings as being made in the image and likeness of God. Hilton writes, 'This is the image that I have spoken of. This – made to the image of God in the first creation — was wonderfully bright and fair, full of burning love and spiritual life, but through the sin of the first man, Adam, it was deformed and changed into another likeness.'[64]

Hilton goes on to describe one of the distinct features of his teaching, 'Since our Lord Jesus – God and man – died thus for the salvation of man's soul, it was just that sin should be forgiven, and that man's soul, which was his image, should be capable of reformation and restoration to the first likeness, and to the bliss of heaven.'[65] Julian, a theologian in her own right, echoes this idea:

> We know by our faith and believe through the teaching and preaching of Holy Church that the blessed Trinity made mankind in its image and in its likeness. In the same way we know that when man fell so deeply and so wretchedly through sin, no other help was forthcoming to restore man except through him who made man. And he who made man for love, by the same love would restore man to the same blessedness and surpassingly more.[66]

Julian, ever the theologian of love, stresses more winsomely and comprehensively than Hilton, that God's action in saving us, in enduring the cross, is an action done out of love, not wrath. A loving sacrifice intended to secure our restoration and transformation. What Hilton calls being 'restored in faith and feeling.' Salvation is no less than saving us from the power of sin and death, but salvation is more. It opens the door for our character, habits, and priorities to be transformed. This is both the hard going and graced rejoicing of the way to Jerusalem.

Margery Kempe: The Weeping Mystic

In 1373, the same year that Julian received her visions, Margery Kempe was born. Richard Rolle had died around 1349, possible of plague. Julian and Hilton were both around thirty years old when Margery was born. Kempe dies sometime after 1439. She, like Julian, lives into the fifteenth century. Margery was born into an influential merchant family in the city of what is now called King's Lynn. In her time, it was called Bishop's Lynn and is located about

fifty miles west of Norwich. It was an important international trading port. Her father, John Brunham, in addition to being a successful merchant, served as mayor of the city and in parliament. Margery married John Kempe, who was also from a merchant family, though not one as influential as her own. Margery's story as we know it comes from her autobiography, *The Book of Margery Kempe*. It is the first known autobiography written by a woman in English. It's not typical of what we would expect of an autobiography because Margery's focus is telling us about her life with God. Nonetheless, the book offers a rare glimpse into the life and thoughts of a medieval woman and her times. The book was lost to history until 1934. An English family who lived in a historic home were playing ping pong. They lost the ball and went looking for a new ball in a nearby cupboard. Instead of a ball, they discovered a book.

Margery was not very interested in God growing up. She was not particularly pious. In her book, she tells us she enjoyed shopping, good food, attractive men, and socializing. She was concerned about her appearance. However, her life took a turn for the worse during her first pregnancy at twenty years of age. It was a very difficult pregnancy. She tells us:

> When this creature was twenty years of age, she was married to a burgess of Lynn, and was with child within a short time,

as nature would have it. And after she had conceived, she was troubled with severe attacks of sickness until the child was born. And then, what with the labour-pains she had in childbirth, and the sickness that had gone before, she despaired of her life, believing she might not live.[67]

Faced with death, Margery was religious enough that she wanted to make a confession. To clear her conscience in case she should die, so she would be prepared to meet God. Her confessor was not patient with her, instead the priest 'began to sharply reprove her before she had fully said what she meant, and so she would say no more in spite of anything he might do.'[68] Following this, Margery had a breakdown, experiencing visions of devils who 'called out to her with great threats, and bade her that she should forsake her Christian faith and belief, and deny God, his mother, and all the saints in heaven, her good works, and all good virtues, her father, mother, and her friends. And so, she did. She slandered her husband, her friends, and her own self.'[69] She even 'bit her own hand so violently that the mark could be seen for the rest of her life'. As a result, 'she was tied up and forcibly restrained both day and night' so that she would not hurt herself or worse.[70] Her family and friends thought she would never recover. She wanted to die. It was then that she experienced a vision:

Our merciful Lord Christ Jesus appeared to his creature who had forsaken him, in the likeness of a man, the most seemly, most beauteous and most amiable that ever might be seen with man's eye, clad in a mantle of purple silk, sitting upon her bedside, looking upon her with so blessed a countenance that she was strengthened in all her spirits, and he said to her these words, 'Daughter, why have you forsaken me, and I never forsook you? And as soon as he had said these words, she saw truly how the air opened as bright as any lightening, and he ascended up into the air, not hastily and quickly, but beautifully and gradually, so that she could clearly behold him

94

in the air until it closed up again. And presently the creature grew as calm in her wits and reason as she ever was before, and asked her husband, as soon as he came to her, if she could have the keys to the buttery to get her food and drink as she had done before. Her keepers advised him that he should not deliver up any keys to her. Nevertheless, her husband, who always had tenderness and compassion for her, ordered that they should give her the keys. And she took food and drink as her bodily strength would allow her, and she once again recognized her friends and household, and everybody who came to her in order to see how Christ had worked his grace in her, who is ever near in tribulation. When people think he is far away from them he is very near through his grace.[71]

Margery recovered and resumed her life. While thankful to God for her recovery, she states that she did not truly know him. She had yet to turn toward Jerusalem. She was proud of her father's accomplishments and her family's social pedigree. She enjoyed the attention of dressing in the most fashionable styles. When people tried to speak to her about her pride, including her husband, she wouldn't listen. On one occasion she tells her husband, John 'that she was come of worthy kindred – he should never have married her – for her father was sometime mayor of the town. Therefore, she would keep up the honour of her kindred, whatever anyone said.'[72] Furthermore, 'She was enormously envious of her neighbours if they were dressed as well as she was. Her whole desire was to be respected by people. She would not learn her lesson from a single chastening experience, nor be content with the worldly goods God had sent her – as her husband was – but always craved more and more.'[73]

She went on to have fourteen children with John Kempe. We don't know if there were fourteen births or fourteen children who survived. The loss of an infant or child was common in the Middle Ages. Life was hard and grief was always nearby, plague or no plague. She also started two businesses, a brewery and a mill. She had some initial success but eventually had difficulty in keeping and attracting employees. In the midst of life as a wife, mother, and business owner, her desire for devotion awakened one evening while in bed with her husband:

> She heard a melodious sound so sweet and delectable that she thought she had been in paradise. And immediately she jumped out of bed and said, 'Alas that ever I sinned! It is fully merry in heaven.' This melody was so sweet that it surpassed all the melody that might be heard in this world, without any comparison, and it caused this creature when she afterwards heard any mirth or melody to shed very plentiful and abundant tears of high devotion, with great sobbings and sighings for the bliss of heaven, not fearing the shames and contempt of this wretched world. And ever after her being drawn towards God in this way, she kept in mind the joy and the melody that there was in heaven, so that so that she could not very well restrain herself from speaking of it.[74]

Margery's conversion to the pilgrim's way had begun. To say that she was enthusiastic was an understatement.

Her enthusiasm was not shared by many of her contemporaries. 'For when she was in company with any people she would often say, 'It is full merry in heaven!' And those who knew of her behaviour previously and now heard her talk so much of the bliss of heaven said to her, 'Why do you talk so of the joy that is heaven? You don't know it and you haven't been there any more than we have.'[75] Margery, who had wanted people to respect her, became an object of ridicule. The ridicule and subsequent controversy grew as the years passed and the miles accumulated on the pilgrimage of her life. Her enthusiasm was part of this, but closely tied to it was her weeping. This began as early as the mystical melody she heard in bed but reached new dimensions when she took to the medieval highways and byways. As a pilgrim, she travelled by way of ship and street, all over England, Europe, and the Middle East. To travel as far as she did on foot or by cart would be remarkable today. For the early fifteenth century, her travels were astonishing, even miraculous in scope. She continued to have visions and communications with Christ throughout her life and in one of these she is instructed to go on pilgrimage to Jerusalem.

After a several-month journey from England, she and a group of pilgrims arrive at the Church of the Holy Sepulchre in Jerusalem:

> The friars lifted up a cross and led the pilgrims about from one place to another where our Lord had suffered his pains and his Passion, every man and woman carrying a wax candle in one hand. And the friars always, as they went about, told them what our Lord suffered in every place. And this creature wept and sobbed as plenteously as though she had seen our Lord with her bodily eyes suffering his Passion at that time. Before her in her soul she saw him in truth by contemplation, and that caused her to have compassion.[76]

Margery wasn't seeing the place where Jesus had been crucified, she was seeing a spiritual vision of Jesus being crucified. 'Before her face she heard and saw in her spiritual sight the mourning of our Lady, of St John and Mary Magdalene, and many others that loved our Lord. And she had such great compassion and such great pain to see our Lord's pain, that she could not keep herself from crying and roaring though she should have died for it. And this was the first crying that she ever cried in any contemplation.'[77]

In the Middle Ages, the gift of tears was widely acknowledged. It was understood as a means of connecting with God and praying for others. The gift of tears was a sign that the Holy Spirit had transformed an individual's heart to love God and love others more deeply and truly. For example, St Dominic, the thirteenth-century founder of the Order of Preachers, was known to weep during the Mass and during his late-night prayer vigils. Margery's weeping, however, was more intense. It was loud and often took place in public, including in church when services were being held. While weeping, she'd sometimes writhe on the floor. She had little control over when these episodes happened and how long they lasted. Some thought she was faking it for attention. Others thought she had a true gift from God. During one period of her life, 'her cries and weeping increased so much that the priests did not dare to give her communion openly in the church, but privately'.[78] Her behaviour divided everyone she met. A typical episode and its effects happened on the Feast of Corpus Christi, which happens annually approximately sixty days after Easter:

> On Corpus Christi Day, as the priests bore the sacrament about the town in solemn procession, with many candles and great solemnity, the said creature followed, full of tears and devotion, with holy thought and meditation, bitter weeping and violent sobbing. And then a good woman came up to this creature and said, 'God give us grace to follow the steps of our Lord Jesus Christ.' Then those words had such an effect in heart and mind that she could not bear it, and had to go into a house. Then she cried out, 'I die, I die,' and roared so astonishly that people were amazed at her, and wondered very much what was wrong with her. And yet our Lord made some people love and cherish her greatly, and invite her home to both eat and to drink, and to have great joy to hear her converse of our Lord.[79]

Margery encouraged the faith of some. They asked for her spiritual guidance and prayers. While she had many such supporters, she also had many detractors, and most numerous, people who were annoyed by her weeping and do-gooding. The path to Jerusalem is seldom a path of popularity. As Jesus experienced in Jerusalem, popularity is often short lived. The crowd that shouts, 'Hosanna to the Son of David' in jubilant welcome one day can shout, 'Crucify him!' in screaming judgment the next (Matthew 19:2; Matthew 22:21). Still,

JULIAN OF NORWICH AND MARGERY KEMPE

Margery must have been a difficult person to be around. Her husband, her friends, her fellow pilgrims, priests, merchants, and maids all reported being exasperated by her. Sometimes her unusual way of life—speaking of God, reprimanding others (including clergy) weeping, and making long pilgrimages without her husband— took her into dangerous territory. The territory of inquisition. Her encounter with the Mayor of Leicester is a good example:

> The Mayor asked her from which part of the country she came, and whose daughter she was. 'Sir,' she said, 'I am from Lynn in Norfolk, the daughter of a good man of the same Lynn, who has been five times mayor of that worshipful borough and I have a good man, also a burgess of the said town of Lynn, for my husband.' 'Ah,' said the Mayor, 'St Katherine told of what kindred she came, and yet you are not alike, for you are a false strumpet, a false Lollard, and a false deceiver of the people, and therefore I shall have you in prison.' And she replied, 'I am as ready, sir, to go to prison for God's love, as you are ready to go to church.'[80]

The encounter escalates from being interrogated by the mayor to being brought before the Bishop of Lincoln. Margery shows herself well formed in the faith, knowledgeable of good doctrine, and courageous in the face of questioning as the only woman in a room full of men – whether government officials, priests, or the Archbishops of York and Canterbury. She even survived the accusations of the Duke of Bedford, John Lancaster, the son of Henry IV. Lancaster was later involved in the trial of St Joan of Arc, who was burned at the stake. Certainly, her father's connections help her, but her faith and her confidence in her mystical experience help her more. Her confidence was in her soul's spouse, Jesus Christ. Christ restored her health and sanity as a young woman and then guided her along her unusual life of travel, prayer, and weeping. Despite her desire for prayer and contemplation, she heeded God's command to be the caregiver of her husband in his incontinent invalid final years and to minister to a young woman, who like she had, experienced a traumatic pregnancy. Near the end of her book, she includes a sampling of her prayers. Her prayers of petition and intercession are wide and comprehensive. She prays for her children, her enemies, the church's leaders, the King, the world's troubles, and those far from God. Her concern is her union with God and her relationship with Christ. Her desire to be united with him in all things. She prays, 'Good Jesus, make my will your will, and your will my will, that I have no will but your will alone.'[81]

Mystic to Mystic: Margery and Walter

Margery tells us in her book that she was familiar with, 'Hilton's book'. This was almost certainly *The Scale of Perfection*. Kempe was a woman who forged her own path of spiritual commitment. In the fourteenth and fifteenth centuries, there was a blossoming lay interest in serious spirituality. Men and women looked to the writings of teachers like Walter Hilton for inspiration and guidance. They sought to apply these writings to their own faith and practice, even though they were not vowed contemplatives. These were people who had spouses, children, and jobs, and, like Margery, desired a deeper life of prayer and devotion. They felt drawn to contemplative life and experience but couldn't pursue such a life according to the traditional means. Hilton helped to open the door to such individuals in his work, *The Mixed Life*. In this book, as we've learned previously, he tells a worldly lord not to abandon his family and responsibilities, but also not to abandon his desire for deeper devotion. Instead, he tells him, 'You must mix the tasks of active life with the spiritual labours of the contemplative life, and then you will do well.'[82] Margery is something of an example of this mixed life. There are some tensions to her remarkable story as it relates to Hilton's order of charity.

For example, her book is largely silent about her fourteen

children. She leaves home for long periods of time without them or her husband, John. She eventually persuades him to give up sex and to live in separate houses. Certainly, wanting to give up sex after having fourteen children is understandable. But for Margery, much of her desire to live without sex is to imitate the lives of vowed contemplatives and to seek union with God alone. She tells us she enjoyed sex with her husband. She also admits she was sexually attracted to another man. However, for her, as for many medieval people, sex was problematic. It was allowed within marriage but was still seen as an arena rife with sin and shame. In spiritual circles, marriage was understood as being inferior to celibacy.

If Hilton had been her spiritual director, he may have instructed her to live a more balanced mixed life. To embrace her active commitments not as obstacles to her faith, but as opportunities to live it out. We are not certain of the balance between her overtly spiritual activities and the rest of her life. Margery's family life is mostly hidden from us, though we do know that she brought a couple of her children with her on a local pilgrimage and that she encouraged her oldest son to greater faith. While there were many devoted Christians who were married in the Middle Ages, the exemplars held up, and those that Margery looked up to, were almost all monastics, living celibate lives. It would take the Protestant Reformation in 1517 to correct this imbalance, restoring marriage to a viable spiritual path. A vocation, a calling, on a par with ordination. Christians before and since Margery have struggled to recognize the human body, sex, and sexuality as treasured gifts, reflecting the goodness of God's creation. It has also been difficult for Christians to play the right set of complementary chords, between honouring marriage, single life, and consecrated life. Our churches and societies would be healthier if all these states and their variations could be seen as viable and mutually edifying ways of being a serious Christian. This would be a good application of Hilton's order of charity.

A PILGRIMAGE OF THE HEART

Mystic to Mystic: Julian and Margery

In the 1410s, Margery, approaching the age of forty and feeling called to a life of greater spiritual commitment, goes to Norwich. Julian, approaching age seventy, has spent long years in prayer and contemplation. Margery tells us, 'She was commanded by our Lord to go to an anchoress called Dame Julian. And so, she did and told her about the grace that God had put into her soul and the converse that our Lord spoke to her along with many wonderful revelations, which she described to the anchoress to find out if there were any deception in them. For the anchoress was an expert in such things and could give good advice.'[83] Julian listens to Margery, as she had listened to many at her window over the years. The result according to Kempe's book,

> The anchoress, hearing the marvellous goodness of the Lord, highly thanked God with all her heart for his visitation, advising this creature to be obedient to the will of our Lord and fulfil with all her might whatever he put into her soul, if it were not against the worship of God and the profit of her fellow Christians. For if it were, then it were not the influence of a good spirit, but rather of an evil spirit. 'The holy Ghost never urges a thing against charity, and if he did, he would be contrary to his own self, for he is all charity.'[84]

Julian in her own book, speaks eloquently of charity: 'So charity keeps us in faith and in hope, and faith and hope lead us in charity. And at the end, all shall be charity.'[85]

Both writers had traumatic illnesses, and both women were healed and brought back from the brink of death and despair by a vision of Jesus Christ. Julian had a spiritual vision of the cross that she spent a lifetime contemplating, leading to her *Revelations of Divine Love*. Margery had many spiritual visions of the cross that repeated throughout her lifetime leading to *The Book of Margery Kempe*. Julian was the first woman to write a book in

JULIAN OF NORWICH AND MARGERY KEMPE

English. Margery was the first woman to write an autobiography in English. Each provided spiritual guidance to others, revealing a God of compassion, intimacy, and grace. Julian spent most of her life in an anchorhold, journeying to the Jerusalem within. Margery spent much of her life on the road, journeying to places near and far, such as Canterbury, Rome, and Jerusalem.

Each woman was persistent. Julian in her revelations persists in questioning God about suffering, sin, grace, and redemption. Margery persists in pursuing her unique version of the mixed life, even in the face of much opposition. Neither Julian nor Margery denies the brokenness of the world. Neither deny the failures of the Church, yet both embrace the Church and encourage all those seeking a serious spiritual life to do so as well. Neither had formal theological education, but both demonstrate theological learning and insight, especially Julian. Despite the bleak situation of their world, their mystical experiences compelled them to proclaim God's courteous love and intimate kindness.

ଏ

It was pouring buckets. A flood watch was announced. Buses and trains were delayed or cancelled. The rain literally looked like a glimmering grey curtain outside the door. I was at St Margaret's in King's Lynn. The home church of Margery Kempe. I was there to give a lecture as part of a special year-long series celebrating the 650th anniversary of Margery's birth, which was also the 650th anniversary of Julian's showings. The rain did not stop. The rector of the church and I wondered what would happen to the lecture. We wondered whether anyone would come. The rain soaked the green gardened grounds of the church. The storm rumbled and roared on the pavements and on the roof. Finally, the rain stopped. The flood warnings abated. It was possible to travel, but would anyone dare to leave their home after that spectacular display? They did. The downpour was a fitting prelude to a talk about a woman who's weeping regularly down poured onto the lives of those around her.

Margery Kempe and Julian of Norwich are the most well-known figures of the English Mystical Tradition, Julian being the most well-known. People are drawn to their mystical experiences and wonder about the curious details of their lives. Through them, men and women around the world have found their hearts encouraged, their faith strengthened, and their humanity normalized and consoled. Mysticism can reach us on our deathbeds and help heal our terrible traumas. Mysticism can weep loudly for the sorrows of the world and sit serenely in the centre of a city. Mysticism can listen at the window and clean the soiled sheets of a spouse. Mysticism has an otherworldly character, but its message of divine love is for our messy lives and our messy world. This is good news.

NEXT STEPS

- Read *Revelations of Divine Love* by Julian of Norwich
- Read *The Book of Margery Kempe*
- Find companions for your journey to Jerusalem.
- Learn about one or more of these topics on your own:
  St Bridget of Sweden   *Ancrene Wise*
  Friends of Julian of Norwich   St Dominic
  The Gift of Tears   The Order of Julian of Norwich
  St Margaret's Church, King's Lynn
- Take a long walk.

JULIAN OF NORWICH AND MARGERY KEMPE

PRAY

'Lord, you say yourself that no one shall come to you without you, nor shall anyone be drawn to you unless you draw them. Therefore, Lord, if there be anyone who is not drawn, I pray you, draw them to yourself.'

Margery Kempe, The Book of Margery Kempe

EXERCISES

Choose one or more exercises to enrich and deepen your learning from this chapter.

- *Contemplate a Cross*

  Silently stand or sit in front of a cross or crucifix for five minutes. The image of the cross is central to the spirituality of the English mystics, and especially to Julian and Margery. Think about the cross. How do you feel contemplating it? What does it make you think of? Does it awaken difficult feelings in you? What about positive feelings? If you feel it is appropriate, pray extemporaneously or with the Lord's Prayer at the end of your five minutes.

- *God as Mother*

  We know that all our language about God is incomplete. Yet, language forms one of the primary ways we relate to God. Experiment with praying to God as Mother. For example, using the Lord's prayer, pray, 'Our Mother who art in heaven.' Also, try praying more conversationally and personally while thinking of God as mother. Take note of your experience and whether you found it difficult, helpful, or something else. We all benefit from using a variety of images for God. The Bible has a wide range of them, as do the prayers and writings of the English mystics.

- *Mary, our Mother*

  Devotion to Mary, mother of Jesus, was second nature to

medieval Christians. This is still true for most Roman Catholic and Orthodox Christians today. For other Christians, the role of Mary in their faith is less certain. Find a picture of Mary and set it before you. Then read the story of the Annunciation to Mary from the Bible found in Luke 1:26-38. Contemplating the picture and the Scripture passage, consider what role Mary has in your spiritual life. Certainly, most Protestant Christians are not going to venerate Mary in the same way Roman Catholic, Anglo-Catholic, and Eastern Orthodox Christians do. Regardless of your tradition and background, how might Mary be a companion with you on the way to Jerusalem?

QUESTIONS

1. What happened to Julian on 13 May 1373? How did that day change her life forever?

2. What do you think about Julian's vision of a hazelnut? How do you understand it? Do you find this vision comforting, perplexing, or something else?

3. Julian was not the first English writer to use mothering language for Christ, but Julian develops this language and a theology around it. What are your thoughts about mothering language for God? What about for Jesus?

4. What were your thoughts and feelings when reading about Margery's first pregnancy and subsequent experiences?

5. Would you want Margery to be a member of your church? Would you want to be friends with her? Why or why not? If you were her pastor, how would you advise her to handle her weeping, especially during worship services?

SIDE TRIP

They say that God lives very high;
But if you look above the pines
You cannot see our God; and why?
And if you dig down in the mines,

JULIAN OF NORWICH AND MARGERY KEMPE

You never see Him in the gold,
Though from Him all that's glory shines.
God is so good, He wears a fold
Of heaven and earth across His face,
Like secrets kept, for love, untold.
But still I feel that His embrace
Slides down by thrills, through all things made,
Through sight and sound of every place;
As if my tender mother laid
On my shut lids her kisses' pressure,
Half waking me at night, and said,
'Who kissed you through the dark, dear guesser?'

Elizabeth Barrett Browning (1860-1861),
A Child's Thought of God

CHAPTER FIVE

MAKING PROGRESS

'This hill, though high, I covet to ascend;
The difficulty will not me offend.'
Pilgrim's Progress

Mapping the Way

Father Martin Thornton, in his book, *English Spirituality,* writes, 'Hilton's system is a usable map, a background against which Christians in all states may safely be guided.' In Walter Hilton's treatise, *Eight Chapters of Perfection,* which predates his masterpiece, *The Scale of Perfection,* he writes, 'There are three ways in which the soul may be transformed.'[86] These stages are common to the Christian mystical tradition. They map the contours of the pilgrimage to Jerusalem for the beginner (the purgative stage), for the proficient (the illuminative stage), and for the perfect (the unitive stage). The purgative stage involves 'following Christ's actions' and seeking to 'resemble him'. In this stage, the pilgrim is a penitent, seeking to get their life in order and figure out the basics of the Christian life. The illuminative stage involves 'awareness of Christ's love' and 'comforts and delights.' In this stage, the pilgrim is a committed disciple, receiving consolation from their faith and making good progress in understanding and living it. The unitive stage involves being 'bound together' and receiving 'joys that cannot be fully expressed in the words of human language'. Here the pilgrim is a lover, abiding with God in intimacy. Hilton describes each stage as a transformation. The pilgrimage to Jerusalem is a journey of change, freely given and received, and hard fought and struggled for. In *The Scale of Perfection*, Hilton has his own way of describing this journey of faith from climbing the lower rungs of character formation to the higher rungs of contemplation. Hilton puts those on the journey to Jerusalem into two categories, those who are 'Reformed in Faith' and those who are 'Reformed in Faith and Feeling'.

Hilton states, 'This reforming is of two kinds: one is in faith alone, and the other is in faith and in feeling. The first, which is reforming in faith alone, is sufficient for salvation; the second is worthy of surpassing reward in the bliss of heaven. The first may be gained easily and in a short time; the second not so, but through length of time and great spiritual labour.'[87] Hilton goes on to tell us, 'The first reforming is only for souls beginning and proficient and for people in active life; and the second is for perfect souls and contemplatives.' While stating this traditional distinction, Hilton also acknowledges God can and does grant contemplation to all sorts and conditions of people. Even if it is vowed contemplatives who most often receive and abide in this gift. In *The Mixed Life,* he adds a third way for those so-called and inclined. A way that may bridge reformation alone with feeling.

Hilton understood the patterns of spiritual pilgrimage mapped out before his time. Hilton also understood, from his own experience on the path and in guiding others along the way, that each person's journey had its own particularities. Spiritual guidance is not a formulaic enterprise, but an art of wisdom drawing upon sound theology, reflective experience, regular prayer, and good sense. Finally, he understood that one stage was never truly left behind. The traditional three stages blend and build upon one another. The classic terms used to describe people in these stages: beginner, proficient, and perfect, make clear that the Christian faith is intended to be a journey of growth and progression. It is a ladder to climb and a pilgrimage to walk. For Hilton, the final stage, that of the perfect, bridges this life to the next. 'Reforming in fullness cannot be had in this life, but it postponed after this life to the glory of heaven.'[88]

Turn, Turn, Turn.

In *The Scale of Perfection*, Hilton encourages his anchoress reader, and all who desire to pursue a serious spiritual life, to turn to God. He writes:

> For you must know that a turning of the body to God, not followed by the heart, is only a figure and likeness of virtues, and not the reality. Therefore any man or woman is wretched who neglects all the inward keeping of the self in order to fashion only an outward form and semblance of holiness, in dress, in speech and in bodily actions; observing the deeds of others and judging their faults; considering himself to be something when he is nothing at all; and so deceiving himself. Do not behave like that but turn your heart together with your body first of all to God, and fashion yourself to his likeness, through humility and charity, and other spiritual virtues; and then you will truly have turned to him.[89]

Turning to God involves inward dispositions and outward behaviours. Hilton calls every baptized Christian to unify these two parts of their lives, not by cultivating appearances of charity and humility, but by becoming charitable and humble. This is part of the active life. The Christian life is more than occasional attendance at worship and more than a commitment to being a generally moral person. Striving, however imperfectly, to be more like Christ is fundamental to the Christian faith. Jesus said, 'If any wish to come after me, let them deny themselves and take up their cross and follow me' (Matthew 16:24). You'll remember that while Margery Kempe had a powerful experience of God after her traumatic pregnancy, she didn't immediately turn to God. Her life went on as it had. It wasn't until sometime later that she turned toward God. Richard Rolle turned to God by dropping out of Oxford and running off into the woods in a makeshift hermit's habit. Turning to God can begin very quietly or very loudly. For Hilton, what is essential in our turning to God is that we do so sincerely and with all our mind, body, and spirit. This kind of turning can take time but the sooner we start the better.

Growth in Christlikeness, cultivating our characters, makes us more ready and able to love our neighbours. Growth in virtue makes us more resilient in the face of life's challenges. It also gives us greater peace of mind and greater capability to deal with and serve others. If Jesus' teachings seem difficult in the Sermon on the Mount and elsewhere, it is because they are. They require God's grace for us to live them fully and faithfully. This is the soul work of rooting out vice and cultivating virtue in our lives. While there are many virtues, Hilton gives priority to the development of humility and charity. Humility not in the sense of unduly putting oneself down, but humility in coming to terms with who you are and not needing to put yourself first. Hilton writes, 'If you think to build a tall house of virtues, first plan for yourself a deep foundation of humility.'[90] Charity not merely in the sense of doing something nice for someone, but in the sense of practising love, the Jesus-like, selfless love of the New Testament.

An Image Problem

The reformation of the soul is difficult because of sin. Hilton teaches that there is a false image that needs to be broken down in the process of reformation and feeling, the image of sin. The image of sin is like a spiritual cataract that blinds us to God and God's activity in the world. The image of sin distorts our natural goodness. This image is in contrast and in opposition to the image humanity was created in by God. In Latin this is called the *imago dei*. The image of God. 'So God created humans in his image, in the image of God he created them, male and female he created them' (Genesis 1:27). This image is associated with Jesus in the New Testament and Christian theology. 'He is the image of the invisible God, the firstborn of all creation; for in him all things in heaven and on earth were created, things visible and invisible, whether thrones or dominions or rulers or powers—all things have been created through him and for him' (Colossians 1:15). Hilton, Julian, and the whole of the English Mystical Tradition stress the importance of humanity being created in the image and likeness of the Triune God. They also affirm the centrality of our relationship with Jesus Christ for knowing God. This belief is foundational in appreciating the spiritual potential of human beings. A potential that can begin to be realized when this image, broken and marred by sin, is restored. Writing to the anchoress, Hilton contrasts these two images:

'This is not the image of Jesus, but it is an image of sin, as St Paul calls it; a body of sin and a body of death. This image and this shadow you carry about with you wherever you go. Many great streams of sin spring out of it, and small ones as well. Just as from the image of Jesus, if it were reformed in you, beams of spiritual light should rise up into heaven – such as burning desires, pure affections, wise thoughts and virtues in all their honour – so from this image spring stirrings of pride, envy, and others like them, which cast you down from the dignity of man into the likeness of a beast.'[91]

The purgative stage of the spiritual life is about dealing with sin, dealing with the stirrings in our lives that drive us away from God and what is good. The illuminative stage is when we begin to experience stirrings that drive us toward God and what is good.

Flood Warning

Hilton goes on to write that 'all sin comes in seven rivers, which are these: pride, envy, wrath, sloth, covetousness, gluttony, and lust. Now this is something you can feel. Every kind of sin runs out by one of these rivers, driving our charity or lessening the fervour of charity.'[92] Hilton identifies pride as the principal river. Pride not in a healthy sense of self-identity, but pride as an exaggerated sense of self. Hilton defines it as 'love of your own excellence, that is, of your own honour'.[93] Hilton teaches that we should actively resist sin and that we should fight vice. 'It is good for a man to have peace with everything except with the devil and with this image of sin, for against them he must always fight – in his thought and in his deed- until he has gained the mastery over them; and that shall never be complete in this life.'[94]

If we don't resist, the rivers of sin will flood the houses of our virtue, polluting our good intentions and actions. In addition to actively resisting sin, he suggests a more positive approach:

> For you must know that someone who has no regard in his desire and his labour for anything other than humility and charity, always craving them, the way to get them and with the work that follows, will in one year, progress and grow more in all other virtues than they would without this desire progress in seven, even though they struggled continually against vice, beating themselves with scourges every day from morning to evening.[95]

Keeping our eyes on Jesus by practising humility and charity is a more fruitful approach to getting to Jerusalem than giving undue attention to our sins. Sin is overcome by God's forgiveness and grace. A grace that is always available for the sincere pilgrim who asks for it. It cannot be cheaply presumed upon but is given by God to those who sincerely lament their failures and mistakes. We cannot overcome sin on our own. God dealt with sin and secured our salvation in the mystery of the life, death, and resurrection of Jesus Christ. Hilton writes, 'However, great a wretch you may be and however much sin you have committed, forsake yourself and your works, good and bad. Cry for mercy and ask only for salvation by virtue of Christ's precious passion, and with trust, and no doubt you shall have it.'[96]

Being reformed in faith is trusting in this salvation. The journey to Jerusalem is the invitation to climb higher, to go further, and, in cooperation with God, to root out sin from our lives and replace it with virtue. Every Christian is called to a life of ongoing confession

MAKING PROGRESS

of sin, turning away from sin, and turning back to God. This is the work of repentance. This is the grace guided cultivation of habits and dispositions that allow the Holy Spirit to bear fruits of virtue in our lives. Fruits that will lead us to take action for others. This emphasis is biblical, 'The fruit of the Spirit is love, joy, peace, patience, kindness, generosity, faithfulness, gentleness, and self-control' (Galatians 5:22-24). Hilton, like most of the great spiritual directors, taught that this character work, was an essential prerequisite for contemplative life and prayer.

❧

Underneath It All

It was a lovely summer's day. I had been to St Peter's Priory Church in Thurgarton many times over the years. I had worshipped there, preached there, prayed there, and more. Located in a small village on the edge of fields and farms, it is in a beautiful spot tucked away in the rural countryside of Nottinghamshire. Sheep and horses are common sights. However, I was excited, because finally, I was going to see parts of the priory I had never seen before. In the fourteenth century, the Augustinian community in Thurgarton was substantial. As a church and centre for spiritual and ecclesial affairs, it rivalled Southwell Minster up the road. Only part of the church that once was is still extant. It's a long story, but eventually after the Reformation in 1517, the priory was restored, not as a monastic house, but as a parish church.

During these subsequent years, new buildings were built on the site of the original priory grounds. Access to the original foundations, the cellar and basement, that go underneath the existing church are only possible through these newer buildings. You must get special permission from the owner of these buildings to access these spaces. The vicar of St Peter's at the time was kind enough to arrange this for me. I was shown around the exquisite grounds and gardens and taken to a door that felt like a portal. A portal that left behind the present and

115

brought us into the past. It was dim and dark as we made our way, walking by the light of our mobile phones. All around us were medieval foundations, rough pillars, and old stonework. I was impressed with how long we walked and how spacious some of the rough shod rooms were. It was all dust and dirt, but sections were separated by stone. It impressed upon me how large the original priory complex must have been in the fourteenth century.

The gentleman who showed me in left me there. I prayed. I pondered. I was in my habit, in the black and white robes of the Dominican Order. If someone else had entered the cellar, they might have mistaken me as a ghost of one of the former occupants of the priory. Over the years, in studying and teaching about the English Mystics, I have noticed a tendency in myself and others to ignore their teachings on grace, sin, virtue, and vice. They considered these teachings foundational for Christian life in general and contemplative life in particular. I suppose the reason that I and others tend to ignore these teachings is because looking into the cellars of our lives is not always pleasant. Furthermore, the process of character growth and reformation, even when graced by God and a supportive community of faith, can be disheartening and slow going. Yet, without foundations, the beautiful edifice of St Peter's Church in Thurgarton wouldn't be standing all these centuries later. Its lovely stained glass, stately interior architecture, and high tower would have collapsed long ago. As we make our way to Jerusalem, we cannot afford to ignore the spiritual and moral foundations of our lives. Without them, we risk jeopardizing our journey and those of others. With due, but not overdue attention to them, we can climb higher with the assurance of having built our spiritual lives on solid ground. Jesus said:

Everyone, then, who hears these words of mine and acts on them will be like a wise man who built his house on rock. The rain fell, the floods came, and the winds blew and beat on that house, but it did not fall because it had been founded on rock. And everyone who hears these words of mine and does not act on them will be like a foolish man who built his house on sand. The rain fell, and the floods came, and the winds blew and beat against that house, and it fell—and great was its fall! (Matthew 7:24-27)

Charity Begins at Home

Hilton and the other English mystics saw the primary responsibility of most Christians, those living the active life, as exercising charity toward their neighbours. This love toward neighbour begins at home and reaches out to the world. This is Hilton's principle of the order of charity. It's why he didn't recommend the worldly lord abandon his family and business responsibilities to become a monk. Instead, Hilton encouraged him to practise his faith within those relationships and responsibilities. One's life is ordered and structured by one's state in life, which in Hilton's time meant whether you were in the world as a layperson, single or married, or had left the world, regular society, and lived as a monastic or solitary.

Alluding to the story of Martha and Mary as symbols of the active and contemplative lives, Hilton writes to the worldly lord in *The Mixed Life*:

> You must be busy with Martha, managing and directing your household, your children, your servants, your neighbours and your tenants; if they do well, support and help them in their work; if they do wrong, teach them to reform, and correct them. You must also find out and take careful heed that your possessions and worldly goods are properly kept by your servants, managed and distributed faithfully, so that you can the more liberally do acts of kindness for your fellow Christians.[97]

The worldly lord is to practise his faith in his daily life. His faith isn't something separate from his daily life, but something integral to it. Through the ups and downs of family life, friendships, work, and societal obligations, he is to practice the virtues, resist sin, and

117

love God by loving his neighbour. Growing in virtue and fighting vice is to take place in the thick of it all, not on a remote island in a monastery. Growth in virtue strengthens those in the active life to live uprightly and to serve others. In writing to the anchoress in *The Scale of Perfection*, Hilton outlines, what we might call today, a ministry and lifestyle for the laity:

> Active life lies in love and charity shown outwardly in good bodily works, in the fulfilment of God's commandments and of the seven works of mercy — bodily and spiritual — toward one's fellow Christians. This way of life belongs to all secular people according to their power and ability, as reason and discretion require; if anyone has a great deal, do a great deal; if he has little, do little, and if he has nothing, then let him have the will to do good. These are the works of the active life, either bodily or spiritual.[98]

A Mission of Mercy

As an individual has the ability and resources, active life consists of practical acts of mercy, love, and assistance to others. These were identified into two groups of seven in the Middle Ages. The works of bodily or corporal mercy and the works of spiritual mercy. The seven-corporal works of mercy are to feed the hungry; give drink to the thirsty, clothe the naked, house the homeless, visit the sick, visit the prisoner, and bury the dead. The seven-spiritual works of mercy are to instruct the ignorant, counsel the doubtful, admonish the sinner, bear wrongs patiently, forgive offences willingly, comfort the afflicted, and pray for the living and the dead.

For Hilton and the wider Christian Tradition, the active life of most Christians is a life of action in the world. Not a life within the walls of a church or monastery. Supporting the active life of every Christian was regular attendance at Mass on Sundays and on special festivals. This was complemented by a basic life of prayer and devotion. Simple prayers were sometimes personal and directed to God conversationally, while others, like the Our Father and Hail

Mary, were recited individually and with others. Instruction in the faith was done by parents for children, and in sermons for adults.

However, instruction by parents was often limited. Also, sound preaching could be difficult to find since most clergy were barely literate and not authorized to preach. This was beginning to change by Hilton's time, thanks in part to the friars' movements started in the thirteenth century by St Francis and St Dominic. The friars, especially the Dominicans, were learned and effective preachers. Margery Kempe highly valued sermons and went out of her way to listen to them. She understood she needed regular instruction in the faith to complement her personal prayer and mystical experiences. In our day of widespread literacy, the reading of devotionals, spiritual books, and the Bible could be added to the practices of the active life. Participation in an occasional retreat, group studies, and online offerings, are also sources of enrichment, instruction, and encouragement for those in active life.

A High Standard

Hilton had a high view of the practice of charity. The implementation of Jesus' commandment, 'You shall love the Lord your God with all your heart, and with all your soul, and with all your mind.' This is the greatest and first commandment. And a second is like it: You shall love your neighbour as yourself.' On these two commandments hang all the law and the prophets' (Matthew 22:34-40). For active life Christians, loving God was done principally in how they lived, morally and spiritually, and how they acted for others in the world. This life of active faith was made possible by participation in the Church and by a rudimentary practice of personal prayer and devotion. The measure of a person's faith was the measure of their charity. Hilton puts it like this in *The Scale of Perfection*:

> There is no difficulty in waking and fasting until your head and body ache, or in going to Rome and Jerusalem on your bare feet, or in rushing about and preaching as if you wanted to convert everybody with your sermons. Neither is it hard to build churches or chapels or feed poor men and make hospitals. But it is a very difficult thing for someone to love his fellow Christians in charity, and wisely to hate his sin, while loving the man. For although it may be true that all the works I mentioned are good in themselves, nevertheless they are common to good men and too bad, for everyone could do them if he wanted to and had the wherewithal. Therefore I regard it as no great feat to do what everyone can do; but to love one's fellow Christians in charity and hate his sin can be done only by good people, who have it by the gift of God and not by their own labour.[99]

Today we can expand Hilton's meaning to 'love your fellow human being'. 'Love them despite their faults.' The challenge is high and difficult, and this speaks to the graced necessity of Spirit-driven growth in our character. There will be people on our pilgrimages we will not be able to love, to show charity toward, without God's assistance. Hilton knew that loving others required God's grace and our efforts to cooperate with that grace. Hilton knew the paradox of charity in the Christian life, he writes, 'There is nothing so hard to acquire as charity. This is true regards your own efforts, but on the other hand I say there is no gift of God that can be had as easily as charity, for our Lord gives no gift as freely, as gladly or widely as he does charity.'[100]

MAKING PROGRESS

Feed the Fire

Hilton is a flexible spiritual guide and director. One essential Hilton stresses, however, is the necessity of feeding the fire of our faith, devotion, and love. There are many ways to do this and what feeds us in one season may not always feed us in another. He emphasizes this teaching in *The Scale of Perfection* with the anchoress in her cell and in *The Mixed Life* with the man of responsibility in the world. *In the Scale,* he ties it directly to his parable of the pilgrim:

> Now that you are on the road and know the name of the place you are bound for, begin to go forward on your journey. Your going forth is nothing else but the work of the spirit – and of the body as well – when there is need for it – which are to use with direction in the following way. Whatever work it is that you should do, in body or in spirit, according to the degree and state which you stand, if it helps this grace-given desire that you have to love Jesus, making it more whole, easier and more powerful for all virtues and all goodness, that is the work I consider best, whether it be prayer, meditation, reading or working; and as long as that task more strengthens your heart and your will for the love of Jesus and draws your affection and your thought, it is good to use it. And if it happens that the savour of it becomes less through use, and you feel that you savour another kind of work more, and you feel more grace in another, take another and leave that one.[101]

In *The Mixed Life*, he compares our desire for God and our feelings of faith to a little coal within our hearts. He writes, 'It works out as if you had a little burning coal with which you wanted to make a fire and get it burning. You would first lay sticks on it and cover the coal; and although it might briefly seem that you were putting the coal out with the sticks, nevertheless after a brief wait, and a little blowing there soon springs out a great flaring flame, for the sticks have turned into fire.'[102] We can assume that we either feel our faith or we don't. We can assume we either have a desire for prayer or we don't. That we have compassion for our neighbour, spouse, or children, or that we don't. Hilton acknowledges that our desire to live our faith can wane, 'It is just so spiritually; the will and desire that you have for God are like a little coal of fire in your soul, for they give you some amount of spiritual heat and light; but very little, since they often grow cold and turn into bodily rest – sometimes into idleness.'[103] Hilton suggests a way to respond to this tendency for the fire of our faith to wane. For the anchoress he recommends she employ a variety of spiritual practices, metaphorical kindling sticks, associated with the contemplative life. With the worldly lord, he recommends, 'put on sticks, which are the good works of active life.' Overall, Hilton's counsel is, 'The more sticks are laid on a fire, the greater is the flame, and so the more varied the spiritual work that anyone has in mind for keeping his desire whole, the more powerful and ardent shall be his desire for God.'[104]

Thankfully, we do not have to be at the mercy of our mood, the troubles of the day, or the difficult seasons of life. Certainly, these, like our sins, can threaten to flood the soul fires in our hearts, but with diligence to the regular patterns of the spiritual life, the consolations we receive from our faith can be regular. Charity toward ourselves and others can grow. The fire within can even burn away our sinful inclinations. The Holy Spirit is the spark of divine love in our hearts. With the wise guidance of spiritual teachers like Hilton and the regular patterns of Christian life, we can generally be assured that our faith will continue to burn brightly. This can be a sign that someone is making progress into the illuminative stage and no longer living only in the purgative stage. Of course, even for the committed disciple and lover of God, there will still be occasions and seasons where their spiritual heart will not burn brightly. Hilton, speaking about this dynamic, encourages the worldly lord not to worry too much if after putting some sticks on the fire of his devotion he doesn't feel inflamed right away.

He encourages him and all of us to persist in our faith. To keep at the work we must do, and the relationships we have, and come back later to our prayers and devotions. Richard Rolle taught that you could have the feeling of God's burning fire continuously. Hilton disagrees, stressing throughout his writings that the grace of devotion, especially higher forms of contemplation, is not regular but intermittent in this life. Whether we feel consolation from our faith or not, Hilton urges us to persist in our regular patterns of personal prayer, Sunday worship, and the like. We are more likely to maintain the flame within if we are in regular contact with people and places that are warm with the spiritual fire of love. If we have no regular practice and no regular contact with people and places that are inflamed with the Spirit, it will be hard for us to be so kindled. In the end, Hilton encourages those spiritual practices that feed our faith and keep it warm and bright. Often with God's grace, if we attend to our inner fire, it will burn steadily even in life's difficult seasons. Then our faith will gift us with warmth and light even in the cold and dark periods of our lives.

Pray Your Way to Jerusalem

'For prayer is nothing but a desire of the heart rising into God' is how Walter Hilton defines prayer in *The Scale of Perfection*. He goes on to describe three kinds of prayer: spoken, personal, and silent. For many on the way to Jerusalem, these three kinds of prayer align with the beginner, proficient, and perfect stages of the spiritual life. Not that pilgrims on the way don't sometimes engage in all three kinds of prayer, but that in each stage, an individual often grows in, develops, and gives more attention to one kind of prayer than the other. Regardless, all three build upon and strengthen one another. For Hilton, you never leave behind one kind of prayer entirely for the other. Since Hilton is writing to an anchoress, he begins with the spoken prayer, which is in fact, the Church's prayer, what we may call today, traditional or liturgical prayer:

> The first is the spoken prayer made specially by God, as is the
> Our Father, and also made more generally by the ordinance
> of holy church, like Matins, Evensongs and the Hours. It is

most useful to say these as devoutly as you can. For when you say your Matins you also principally say your Our Father, and to stir you to more devotion it was further laid down that psalms, hymns, and other similar pieces made by the Holy Spirit should be said as well. Therefore, you should not say them greedily or carelessly as if you resented being tied to them, but you shall collect your affection and your thought to say them more steadfastly and more devoutly than another other special prayer of devotion.[105]

Today, this principle could be applied to the prayers we say at home according to traditional patterns, like a grace at meals. It can also be applied to when we attend worship, avoiding the temptation to participate in the service, whatever its format, traditional or contemporary, in a perfunctory manner.

This applies also to those who, like Hilton and Ignotus, were obliged to pray the Church's daily cycle of prayers, known as the Daily Office or The Liturgy of the Hours. Matins and Evensong are two of those daily services. Anchoresses like Julian and hermits like Richard Rolle also prayed a version of these. Margery Kempe also says that she sometimes prayed this form of prayer, though she was not obligated to. Hilton refers to the Daily Office in a special way, 'a person needs a firm staff to hold him up if he cannot run easily by spiritual prayer because his feet are infirm through sin. This staff is the special spoken prayer ordained by God and holy church to help people's souls.'[106] Today, many people across the world, who are not obliged to pray these services, pray with benefit some version of them every day. The four principal services being Morning Prayer, Noonday Prayer, Evening Prayer and Compline. Certain churches, especially cathedrals, as well as monastic communities, maintain and offer this daily cycle of prayer. By doing so they help hold up themselves, the Church, and the world.

Moving on, Hilton says, 'The second kind of prayer is spoken, but without any particular words, and this is when a man or woman feels the grace of devotion, by the gift of God, and in his devotion speaks to him as if he were bodily in his presence.'[107] For many Christians, this is the most familiar kind of prayer. It is personal and often consists of informal petitions, intercessions, and thanksgiving. Personal prayer prayed throughout the week complements more formal prayer offered on Sunday. Personal prayer can sometimes take on a more contemplative dimension, where a person feels, 'so much goodness, grace, and mercy in God that he is glad to praise and thank him with greater affection from the heart and praise our Lord by such words he is stirred to say'.[108]

The third kind of prayer is a form of contemplation, deeper prayer. Hilton says, 'the third kind of prayer is only in the heart, without speaking and with great rest of body and soul'.[109] This kind of prayer is closer to the realm of what Ignotus teaches in *The Cloud of Unknowing*. This kind of prayer is traditionally associated with the unitive stage of mystic journeying. Complementing all three kinds of prayer, especially in preparation for silent prayer, would be the practice of *lectio divina*, sacred reading. Sacred reading is a form of meditative reading of Scripture. In addition, as we progress further toward Jerusalem, worship services on Sundays and other occasions can begin to take on more meditative and contemplative dimensions. There is a deep end to experience in the spiritual pool of Christian worship. This is especially true, according to the tradition of Christian mystics, of the Eucharist.

At all stages of the spiritual life, distractions can be an issue. Hilton writes to the anchoress:

> For when you want to have the intention of your heart held upward to God in prayer, you feel so many vain thoughts of the things you have done or will do, or of other people's actions, with many other such matters in hindering and vexing you, that you can feel neither savour nor rest in your prayer nor devotion in what you are saying. And often the more you labour to control your heart, the further it is from you, and sometimes the harder from the beginning to end, so that you feel everything you is merely lost.[110]

In response to the challenge of distractions, Hilton recommends that we begin every prayer time with a firm intention:

> When you are about to pray, make your intention and your will at the beginning as complete and as pure toward God as you can, briefly in your mind, and then begin to do as you can. And however badly you are hindered from your first resolve, do not be too fearful, or too angry with yourself, or impatient against God for not giving you that savour and spiritual sweetness with devotion which (as it seems to you) he gives to other creatures. Instead, see by it your own weakness and bear it easily, holding your prayer in your own sight with humbleness of heart, and trusting confidently in the mercy of our Lord that he will make it good — more than you know or feel; and if you do so, all shall be well.[111]

The important thing according to Hilton and many teachers of prayer is to keep at it. To stress his point Hilton adds, 'Though you fall in the same way another time — yes — a hundred times, a thousand times! Still do as I have said, and all shall be well.'[112] Prayer in the English Mystical Tradition is a prayer that persists, however lofty, however simply, however focused, however distracted.

Obstacles on the Road

Hilton recognizes the traditional three-fold enemies of the spiritual life. The flesh, the devil, and the world. The flesh is the image of sin within us. The devil being Satan and all the spiritual forces that oppose God. Margery and Julian both encountered demonic opposition. The world being the systems, forces, and ways around us which work against the systems, forces and ways of the Kingdom of God. In relation to his parable of the pilgrim and the threats of enemies, Hilton gives principal attention to the enemies that come from within:

Now that you are on the way and know how you shall go. Beware of enemies that will be trying to hinder you if they can, for their intention is to put out of your heart that desire and longing that you have for the love of Jesus and to drive you home again. These enemies are principally sinful desires and vain fears that rise out your heart. Whether your thoughts or unclean spirits you have one remedy. Whatever it may be that they say, do not believe them, but keep on your way and desire only the love of Jesus. Always give this answer: I am nothing; I have nothing; I desire nothing but the love of Jesus alone. If your enemies speak in your heart, that you have not made a proper confession, or that there is some old sin hidden in your heart that you do not know and never confessed, and therefore you must turn home again, leave your desire and go make a better confession, do not believe this saying, for it is false and you are absolved. Similarly if they say you are not worthy to have the love of God, do not believe them, but go forward. Trust firmly that you are on the road, and you need no more ransacking of your confession for what is past; keep on your way and think of Jerusalem.[113]

When dealing with difficulties like these, Hilton recommends the anchoress take appropriate action according to the counsel of her spiritual director. Obstacles on the road to Jerusalem are best met in the company with other wayfarers, not alone.

Don't Try So Hard

The writings of many medieval saints, mystics, and teachers of prayer strike us as severe. Much of our perception is due to the tremendous cultural differences between the fourteenth century and our own. Yet, some medieval practices were too severe and seemed to lack an appropriate Christian understanding of the value of the body and the priority of grace. Other practices ignored the importance of love, for self, for others, and for God. Nonetheless, one of the hallmarks of Hilton's guidance is his emphasis on moderation.

To the anchoress he writes, 'For with regard to your bodily nature, it is good to use discretion, in eating, drinking and sleeping, and in every kind of bodily penance either in prolonged vocal prayer or in bodily feeling from great fervour of devotion — as in weeping or the like — and in spiritual imagining as well when one feels no grace. In all these kinds of work it is good to keep discretion, perhaps by breaking off sometimes; for moderation is best.'[114] Throughout his writings, he encourages his readers to not force their prayers but to take their time. Hilton encourages his readers to take breaks from spiritual activities. This allows them to come back to them feeling refreshed. Rest is important. The road to Jerusalem cannot be rushed. Our progress on the path only happens with God's help. Hilton writes, 'Nobody is suddenly made perfect in grace, but through long exercise and skilled working a soul may come to it. For no soul can come to it without help from the Spirit.'[115]

Contemplation: General and Technical

In the Christian Spiritual Tradition, the word contemplation is often used as a general term for prayer, spiritual reflection, and related activities. There is also the technical use of the word contemplation, which Hilton defines as having three parts or degrees:

> The first part is the knowledge of God and the things of the spirit, acquired by reason, by the teachings of man and the study of holy scripture without the spiritual affection or inward savour felt by the Holy Spirit. This part belongs especially to learned persons and great scholars who by long study and labour in holy scripture come to this knowledge — more, or less, according to the subtly of their natural wit and perseverance in study, upon the basis of the general gift given by God to everyone who has the use of reason. This knowledge is good, and it may be called a part of contemplation.[116]

MAKING PROGRESS

The first part of contemplation is the experience of study. Describing the second part, Hilton states, 'The second part of contemplation lies principally in affection.'[117] This is the contemplation experience of devotion, of feeling sweetness and edification in prayer. Finally, Hilton describes the third part as follows:

> The third part of contemplation, which is as perfect as can be here lies both in cognition and affection, that is to say, in the knowing and perfect loving of God. That is when a person's soul is first cleaned from all sins and reformed in the image of Jesus by completeness of virtues and is illumined by the grace of the Holy Spirit to see the Truth, which is God, with a soft sweetly burning love for him so that for a time he is united and conformed to the image of the Trinity. The beginning of this contemplation may be felt in this life, but fullness of it is kept in the bliss of heaven.[118]

In this book, we have seen examples of these higher forms of contemplation in the mystical experiences spoken of by Richard Rolle, *The Cloud of Unknowing* author, Julian of Norwich, and Margery Kempe. The practices leading up to and including various forms of contemplation have helped to sustain the witness of the Church for centuries. Contemplative life contributes to the Church's ongoing prayer for the world, the Church's spiritual vitality in worship, and energizes the Church's service to those in need. There is indeed gold in the hills of the Christian faith. Gold that does not always glitter, but by the power of the Holy Spirit, warms the hearts of the faithful, and inspires those far from God to seek the way to Jerusalem.

Contemplation Who Cares?

Most Christians can appreciate the value of contemplative spirituality and of certain contemplative practices. However, some people struggle to see the value of the contemplative life in its traditional expressions, such as that lived by cloistered monks and nuns. When

A PILGRIMAGE OF THE HEART

I was teenager and discerning a call to a particular religious order, my mother was terribly concerned I'd join one of those orders that, to use her language, 'only prays'. She said it would be a waste of my life. I begged to differ then, and I beg to differ now.

The Holy Spirit works through the whole Body of Christ, and outside of the visible Body of Christ, to accomplish God's purposes for the world. No one person, church, or ministry, can embody the fullness of the spiritual life. Contemplatives hold up for the rest of us the hidden life of Christ in the desert, on the mountain, and in quiet places praying. Their sheer existence is an invitation and provocation for the rest of us to consider what is important in life and in our own lives. Their existence challenges us to give more attention to matters of the Spirit. The prayers of contemplatives benefit us all. Their hidden life - the life of ceaseless prayer offered by a monk, nun, or contemplative person outside formal structures - ignites a bright flame of love, a twinkling star, into the world. The world is made brighter and warmer by their prayers.

Archbishop Desmond Tutu, the famed South African bishop and theologian, who received the Nobel Peace Prize for his work in opposing Apartheid in South Africa, was a man of action. He dedicated his long life to the pursuit of justice, of enacted and visible charity toward his neighbours. Many of his accomplishments are widely known, what is not widely known, is that he was an oblate of the Order of Julian of Norwich. The Order of Julian of Norwich is a small monastic community of Episcopal nuns in Wisconsin in the United States. The nuns follow the teachings of Julian, committing themselves to the work of liturgical and corporate prayer and to a life of contemplative and silent prayer.

Oblates of the order come from a variety of Christian denominations and adopt a practice of silent prayer in affiliation with the nuns. In 2011, Mother Hilary, the superior of the order, wrote privately to Archbishop Tutu about her vision of the order embracing their contemplative calling at an even deeper level by being more like Julian. Here, with her permission, is how Archbishop Tutu replied:

MAKING PROGRESS

What you want is what we desperately need, those who almost ceaselessly hold us up and all of God's creation bringing us into the ambit of the throne of grace, to be there in our stead offering praise and adoration, contrition and tears for our sins and of the many who never think they should say sorry to God or their hapless victims, holding, bearing up before God, God's world aching so much, those skeletons that are Somali children, the victims of injustice and oppression, the girls and women raped where rape is weapon of war, to degrade and dehumanise them, and hold up the perpetrators for they too are God's children. Without you to do and be this, our world is doomed. Oh, how much we need you to be this only with no distractions however worthy. We need you to be this desperately. Please be. It is a tough call but we are doomed if you do not follow the promptings of your heart, the movement of the Spirit.

NEXT STEPS
- Read *The Scale of Perfection*
- Read *The Epistle on the Mixed Life*
- Rest. Take a break. Play or watch some sport.
- Learn about one or more of these topics on your own:
  Purgative Way   Illuminative Way   Unitive Way
  Contemplation   Imago Dei   Liturgical Prayer   Daily Office
- Get serious about making my way to Jerusalem.

PRAY
'My Lord God, I have no idea where I am going. I do not see the road ahead of me. I cannot know for certain where it will end.

A PILGRIMAGE OF THE HEART

Nor do I really know myself, and the fact that I think that I am following your will does not mean that I am actually doing so. But I believe that the desire to please you does in fact please you. And I hope I have that desire in all that I am doing. I hope that I will never do anything apart from that desire. And I know that if I do this you will lead me by the right road, though I may know nothing about it. Therefore, will I trust you always, though I may seem to be lost and in the shadow of death. I will not fear, for you are ever with me, and you will never leave me to face my perils alone.'

Thomas Merton, *Thoughts on Solitude*

EXERCISES
Choose one or more exercises to enrich and deepen your learning from this chapter.

- *A Heart Examen*

  Give yourself seven minutes of quiet. Have a pen and piece of paper or other means of capturing your thoughts. *In The Scale of Perfection* Hilton writes, 'For what is a man but his thoughts and his loves?' He goes on to say, 'If you want to know what you love, look at what you think about; for where love is, there is the eye, and where the pleasure is, there is the heart thinking most. If you love God greatly, you will like to think about him a great deal; and if you love him little, then you will give him little thought.' Without judgment write down who or what you think about most days and who or what you spend most of your time looking at most days. What does this examination reveal to you about what you love, about what's important to you, and about your relationship with God? Hilton's exercise is reminiscent of Jesus' words, 'For where your treasure is, there your heart will be also' (Matthew 6:12).

- *Have You Turned?*

  Take five minutes to answer the question of whether you have turned to God. Have you turned in the way that Hilton describes? How long do you think it would take you to turn in this way? Write down areas of your life where you have made good progress in turning to God and areas of your life where you have made less progress in turning to God. Finally, consider whether there were times in your life when you turned away from God. What were these times like and did you eventually turn back to God?

QUESTIONS

1. What do you think about categories of growth for the spiritual life? For example, the three-fold journey of purgation, illumination, and union or about Hilton's categories of 'Reformed in Faith' and 'Reforming in Feeling?' How can such categories be useful and how can such categories be problematic?

2. Walter Hilton, like many other teachers of prayer, stressed the importance of dealing with personal sin and growing in personal virtue. Does this make sense to you? How might our prayer and the content of our character be related?

3. What did you think about Hilton's teaching on fire and sticks? Does this teaching suggest anything you need to do differently in your faith journey? Does this teaching have any implications for how churches seek to support the spiritual lives of their members?

4. Walter Hilton outlines three kinds of prayer. What are these? Have you tried all of them? When praying on your own, which of the three do you most use? How might you begin to use all three types of prayer more regularly, or if you already do, in a different way?

5. What is the value of prayer? More specifically, what about contemplative prayer and those individuals who give their lives to its practice? If a friend, child, or relative were wanting to give themselves principally to prayer, either as a nun or monk, or by using the majority of their free time or retirement for prayer, how would you respond to them?

A PILGRIMAGE OF THE HEART

SIDE TRIP

O God the Holy Ghost
Who art light unto thine elect
Evermore enlighten us.
Thou who art fire of love
Evermore enkindle us.
Thou who art Lord and Giver of Life,
Evermore live in us.
Thou who bestowest sevenfold grace,
Evermore replenish us.
As the wind is thy symbol,
So forward our goings.
As the dove, so launch us heavenwards.
As water, so purify our spirits.
As a cloud, so abate our temptations.
As dew, so revive our languor.
As fire, so purge our dross

Christina Rossetti (1830-1894),
A Prayer to the Holy Spirit

CONCLUSION

An Invitation to a Deeper Life

In her book, *The Mystics of the Church,* Evelyn Underhill writes, 'Mysticism has been defined as 'the science of the Love of God',[119] and certainly those words describe its essence. But, looking at it as it appears in the Christian Church in all its degrees and forms, I would prefer to call it 'the life which aims at union with God.' These terms – life, aim, union – suggest its active and purposive character; the fact that true Christian mysticism is neither a philosophical theory nor a name for a delightful religious sensation, but that is a life with an aim, and this aim is nothing less than the union of man's spirit with the very Heart of the Universe.' It has been the purpose of this book to encourage you in the pursuit of this life, to make your life a pilgrimage, a pilgrimage of the heart.

Walter Hilton, Richard Rolle, Ignotus, Julian of Norwich, and Margery Kempe have pointed the way for us toward Jerusalem. They have offered their wisdom, experience, and insight. Hilton has warned us about challenges, given us guidance for problems, and urged us to keep our fires kindled and our eyes on the destination. Along the way, we crossed paths with several other sojourners. We have met saints, scholars, mystics, poets, theologians, and writers. They are representative of the countless pilgrims who have made this very divine and yet very

135

human journey. The English mystics, for all their individuality and peculiarity, understood their lives and their faith were part of a larger whole. They knew they did not walk alone. They lived within these verses: 'Since we are surrounded by such a great cloud of witnesses, let us throw off everything that hinders and the sin that so easily entangles. And let us run with perseverance the race marked out for us, fixing our eyes on Jesus, the pioneer and perfecter of faith' (Hebrews 11:1-2).

Christian mysticism is never a solitary affair, even for a hermit by himself in the woods. Mysticism is a shared ecosystem of the Spirit. An ecosystem harmonized and united by God and grown in human souls across space and time. The exuberance of Rolle, the hiddenness of Ignotus, the assurance of Julian, the insistence of Margery, and the wisdom of Hilton point us toward and invite us into this ecosystem of the Spirit. An ecosystem where God grows us and invites our participation in our growth. We are not passive. We can respond and open the door of our hearts to the great mystery. Yet, everything we gain, even the hardest that we fight for, is ultimately a gift. This is why our companion mystics in this volume were people of profound gratitude. Genuine mysticism always gives thanks.

The Craft of Contemplation

The mystery of the Christian faith is that ultimate reality became human reality. St John, the most mystical of the four Gospels, states this mystery directly, 'The Word became flesh and lived among us' (John 1:14). Contemplation, another name for the mystic experience and the life related to this experience, is the experience of this verse. The experience of God's reality, God's Word, God's Son, God's Spirit, becoming poured into our hearts and our lives. This pouring of divine power, grace, and love into all of our human brokenness and all of our God-given human potential can transform us into lovers of God. This will necessarily turn us into lovers of people, even the most difficult kinds of people. This isn't easy. If it were, Walter Hilton and countless other spiritual directors and theologians over the

CONCLUSION

centuries wouldn't have written books to guide themselves and others in this 'science of love.' Hilton suggests that loving God and loving others is like a craft. A craft we must learn by apprenticing ourselves to those who have made further progress than we have. In this life, apprentices or journeymen, we all sit at the feet of the master lover, the carpenter from Galilee.

A craft whose practice, by God's grace and by our graced efforts, we should improve in, sometimes haltingly, sometimes painfully, over the years of our pilgrimage. Not as a way of earning anything, because everything is a gift, but as a way of becoming fully alive. Hilton writes, 'Of all crafts that there are, the service of God is the most excellent and subtle, the highest and the hardest to reach in its perfection, and also it is the most profitable and the most gainful for one who can truly practice it.'[120] The craft that Hilton has in mind is the practice of charity. The practice of loving God and loving others. For Hilton, the mountaintop mystical love of God cannot leave behind the flat field day-in and day-out love of other human beings. Hilton quotes Jesus' words, 'This is my commandment, that you love one another as I have loved you' and expands on them, 'For people shall know you are my disciples; not because you work miracles, cast out devils, or preach and teach, but if you love one another in charity.'[121]

In So Many Words

Many years ago, as a young man, I wrote this poem.

Where have you gone?
What have you seen?
If you can, catch some words and send them to me.
Words are pretty things,
though shadows they may be.
The truest thing is the sight seen.
Yet, I will take your words to my open heart,
they will be sight enough for me.

A PILGRIMAGE OF THE HEART

You have heard the words of a variety of people in this volume. You have heard where the mystics have gone and what the mystics have seen. Even when well given, their words are cataphatic shadows. Nonetheless, I hope that you have taken the words of the English mystics, and at least some of mine, to your open heart. For many believers, the experiences of the English mystics, and saints like them, are a witness to and confirmation of their own Christian faith. For some people, it is enough that someone else has made their way to Jerusalem and experienced the things of God. The lives of the mystics are burning flames, kindled by the Spirit, that help light the soul fires of us all.

Michael Ramsey, the 100th Archbishop of Canterbury, put it this way: 'The saint is one who has a strange nearness to God, and makes God real and near to other people.' The English Mystics are a motley mix of strangeness and nearness to God. Their particularities have helped make God real and near to many pilgrims over the centuries. Yet, the invitation of the saints and mystics, the friends and lovers of God, across the denominations of the Christian faith, is not, 'look at me' but 'come and see.' They urge you to go, to see, and to make your own way to Jerusalem. They will accompany you as you make your way, but you must open the door of your life and get going. Then you will have your own words to share. Words born of progress and pitfall on the pilgrimage of life.

ॐ

An Unseen Shore

A few years ago, after having been in Thurgarton at the Priory Church of St Peter, I went on a preaching mission that eventually brought me to Scotland. It was autumn, with its leaves of gold and brown, and with Britain's usual weather, grey and rain. I preached to a congregation of St Paul's Cathedral in Dundee. This Sunday service was my final preaching commitment of the trip, having been on the road for two weeks. I stayed chatting with worshippers until almost everyone had gone. The people were kind and welcoming. The provost of the cathedral, the head priest, and his family were especially hospitable. Just as I was making my way out the door of the now- empty church, a woman came up to me and placed a shell in my hand. I had never met the woman before and had little conversation with her that morning. I do not recall her name, but I do remember she was helping with the service as a lay reader. She told me the shell was from St Columba's Bay, which is located off the island of Iona, on the west coast of Scotland. Iona has been a holy place and a destination for pilgrims for centuries. She said, 'I have made my pilgrimage to Iona. Now, I am passing this shell on to you. Someday, after you have been there, you can pass it on to someone else.'

I have yet to see the holy island. I hope someday to make a pilgrimage there. I keep the shell in my personal devotional space, next to a stone from the churchyard at Thurgarton. Consider this book to be its own seashell, pulled from the blessed bay of the deep wisdom of the English mystics. They have much more to show you than I have shown you in this little volume. You must befriend them yourself. Read their writings, talk with their friends, love their God, and follow their saviour. In this holy pilgriming you will grow. You will find the fire of your faith kindled. Kindled when life is grand and glorious, the mountain top highs. Kindled when life is dim and discouraged, the valley bottoms. Often life is more humdrum, a simple walk between the valleys and mountains. In this daily walk are simple joys, tedious necessities, and quiet sorrows. The spiritual life is meant to be lived throughout all this terrain, not just during occasional trips to a splendid shrine in the hills. A life where we discover that everyday can have its own divine beauty, winsome goodness, and illuminating truth.

Ever Ancient and Yet Ever New

The contemplative path has in the main, not changed. It is now available to more people than in the Middle Ages because of widespread literacy, giving people access to the right guides and resources. It is also available to more people today because of a renewed understanding of the call of all baptized Christians to a serious and devout life. A life that may include aspects of both the active and contemplative lives. A new kind of mixed life for the present century. A life that is full of joy. A life which can include, as Julian reveals to us in her showings, laughter. Over our forebears we have the advantages of the social and natural sciences in complementing our spiritual understanding of human beings and the world. To our disadvantage is the fact we live in societies that do not value God and the things of God. This means we must attend carefully to creating spiritual enclosures for ourselves that kindle the fires of our hearts. Technology is a blessing and a bane in this pursuit. Contemplation requires focused attention. Technology often distracts us from giving attention to who and what is most important.

Mysticism is one of the unique dimensions of human experience. It is an organic experience of the human person in relationship to God and all God has created. A new asceticism, building upon the early asceticism of the desert fathers and mothers, the English mystics, and our more recent ancestors in the faith, will increasingly be needed for our time. A new asceticism, a graced form of self-denial, that Christians must cultivate to strike the right balance between technological engagement and human wholeness. There are no shortcuts to genuine mysticism. This is because genuine mysticism is intended to facilitate the transformation of our lives. In other words, the transformation of our characters, priorities, and pursuits. Anyone can have an unusual spiritual experience that is memorable, even exhilarating. The long haul of the journey to Jerusalem is a mysticism of love. A love that struggles, grows, transforms, and restores.

Trust you are called to this path. Find companions for the way. Persist when the way is hard. Lean on the grace of God. Carry your staff of prayer. Be not afraid. Remember all that is gold does not glitter. Listen to the whisper and melody of the Spirit. Ignore the distractions and distractors. Find the true treasures at the heart of the Church's life. Do not let church leaders forget about them or how to find them. More than anything, put one foot in front of the other, one prayer prayed after the other, and one loving act done after the other. Make your life a pilgrimage. Be blessed. Be a blessing. 'May the grace of the Lord Jesus Christ, and the love of God, and the fellowship of the Holy Spirit be with you' (1 Corinthians 13:14).

REFERENCES

1   Joan M. Nuth, *God's Lovers in an Age of Anxiety: The Medieval English Mystics* (London: Darton, Longman and Todd, 2001), 27.

2   E. A. Jones, ed. *The Medieval Mystical in England: Exeter Symposium VII* (Woodbridge: D.S. Brewer, 2013), 129.

3   Walter Hilton, *Epistola ad quemdam seculo reninciari*, in *Walter Hilton's Latin Writings*, ed. John P.H. Clark and Cheryl Taylor, vol 2. (Salzburg, Austria: Institut Fur AnglisTik Und Amerikanistik Universitat, 1987).

4   Anne Savage and Nicholas Watson, trans. *Anchorite Spirituality: Ancrene Wisse and Associated Works* (New York: Paulist Press, 1991).

5   Walter Hilton, *De imagine peccati* in *The Cambridge Companion to Medieval English Mysticism*, eds. Samuel Fanous and Vincent Gillespie (Cambridge: Cambridge University Press, 2011), 121.

6   Hilton, *De imagine peccati*, 77.

7   Bernard McGinn, *The Varieties of Vernacular Mysticism: 1350-1500* (New York: Crossroad, 2012), 381.

8   David Knowledges, *The English Mystical Tradition* (New York: Harper and Brothers, 1961), 104.

9   Julia Gatta, *Three Spiritual Directors for our Time* (Cambridge, MA: Cowley Publications, 1986), 17.

10 McGinn, *The Varieties of Vernacular Mysticism*, 374.

11 McGinn, 377.

12 Walter Hilton, *Mixed Life*, trans. Rosemary Dorward (Oxford:

SLG Press, 2001).

[13] Hilton, *Mixed Life*, 5–6.

[14] McGinn, *The Varieties of Vernacular Mysticism*, 372–73.

[15] Walter Hilton, *The Scale of Perfection*, eds. John Clark and Rosemary Dorward (New York: Paulist, 1991), 227.

[16] Dee Dyas, *The Dynamics of Pilgrimage: Christianity, Holy Places, and Sensory Experience* (New York: Routledge, 2022), 1.

[17] Hilton, *The Scale of Perfection*, 227–28.

[18] Jennifer Hillman and Elizabeth Tingle, eds., *Soul Travel: Spirituality Journeys in Late Medieval and Early Modern Europe* (Oxford: Peter Lang, 2019), 1.

[19] Walter Hilton, *The Mixed Life*, trans. Rosemary Dorward (Oxford: SLG Press, 2001), 6.

[20] Hilton, *The Mixed Life*, 6.

[21] Hilton, 6.

[22] Hilton, 6.

[23] Hilton, 6.

[24] Hilton, 6.

[25] Bernard McGinn, *The Varieties of Vernacular Mysticism: 1350-1550* (New York: Crossroad, 2012), 340.

[26] Richard Rolle, *The Fire of Love*, trans. Clifton Wolters (Harmondsworth, Middlesex: Penguin Books, 1972), 9.

[27] Joan M. Nuth, *God's Lovers in an Age of Anxiety: The Medieval English Mystics* (London: Darton, Longman and Todd, 2001), 40.

[28] Richard Rolle, *The Fire of Love*, trans. Clifton Wolters (Harmondsworth, Middlesex: Penguin Books, 1972), 93.

[29] Rolle, *The Fire of Love*, 45.

[30] Rolle, 191.

[31] Rolle, 189–9.

[32] Hilton, *The Scale of Perfection*, 84.

[33] I first encountered this way of referring to *The Cloud* Author by listening to a talk by James Finley.

[34] Walsh, James, ed., *The Cloud of Unknowing* (Mahwah, NJ: Paulist, 1981), 101.

REFERENCES

35 *The Cloud of Unknowing*, 101.

36 *The Cloud of Unknowing*, 119.

37 *The Cloud of Unknowing*, 128.

38 *The Cloud of Unknowing*, 157.

39 *The Cloud of Unknowing*, 145.

40 For example, 'keen shaft'. See William Johnson, *The Mysticism of the Cloud of Unknowing* (New York: Fordham, 2000), 55. See also, Wolfgang Riehle uses 'the image of a sharp arrow.' Wolfgang Riehle, *The Secret Within: Hermits, Recluses, and Spiritual Outsiders in Medieval England* (Ithaca, NY: Cornell University Press, 2014), 161 .

41 *The Cloud of Unknowing*, 153.

42 *The Cloud of Unknowing*, 218.

43 *The Cloud of Unknowing*, 134.

44 *The Cloud of Unknowing*, 134.

45 *The Cloud of Unknowing*, 134.

46 *The Cloud of Unknowing*, 249.

47 *The Cloud of Unknowing*, 185.

48 *The Cloud of Unknowing*, 202.

49 *The Cloud of Unknowing*, 203.

50 *The Cloud of Unknowing*, 239.

51 *The Cloud of Unknowing*, 187.

52 Julian of Norwich, *Revelations of Divine Love*, trans. Barry Windeatt (Oxford: Oxford University Press, 2015), 42.

53 Anne Savage and Nicholas Watson translators. *Anchorite Spirituality: Ancrene Wisse and Associated Works* (New York: Paulist Press), 201.

54 Julian of Norwich, *Revelations of Divine Love*, 7.

55 Julian of Norwich, 45.

56 Julian of Norwich, 115.

57 Julian of Norwich, 130.

58 Julian of Norwich, 133.

59 Julian of Norwich, 126.

60 Julian of Norwich, 133.

61 Julian of Norwich, 130.

62 Julian of Norwich, 160.

63 Julian of Norwich, 78.

64 Hilton, *The Scale of Perfection*, 193.

65 Hilton, 195.

66 Julian of Norwich, *Revelations of Divine Love*, 54.

67 Margery Kempe, *The Book of Margery Kempe*, trans. Barry Windeatt (London: Penguin Classics, 2019), 11.

68 Kempe, *The Book of Margery Kempe*, 11.

69 Kempe, 11.

70 Kempe, 12.

71 Kempe, 12–13.

72 Kempe, 13.

73 Kempe, 14.

74 Kempe, 15–16.

75 Kempe, 16.

76 Kempe, 70–71.

77 Kempe, 71.

78 Kempe, 141.

79 Kempe, 110.

80 Kempe, 113.

81 Kempe, 253.

82 Hilton, *The Mixed Life*, 6.

83 Kempe, *The Book of Margery Kempe*, 45.

84 Kempe, 46.

85 Julian of Norwich, *Revelations of Divine Love*, 163.

86 Walter Hilton, *8 Chapters on Perfection and Angel's Song*, trans. Rosemary Dorward (Oxford: SLG, 1992), 11.

87 Hilton, *The Scale of Perfection*, 199.

88 Hilton, 198.

89 Hilton, 77.

90 Hilton, 91.

91 Hilton, 124.

92 Hilton, 126.

93 Hilton, 127.

94 Hilton, 208.

REFERENCES

[95] Hilton, 148.

[96] Hilton, 114.

[97] Hilton, *The Mixed Life*, 6.

[98] Hilton, *The Scale of Perfection*, 78.

[99] Hilton, 137.

[100] Hilton, 138.

[101] Hilton, 229.

[102] Hilton, *The Mixed Life*, 16.

[103] Hilton, 16.

[104] Hilton, *The Scale of Perfection*, 230.

[105] Hilton, 99.

[106] Hilton, 99.

[107] Hilton, *The Scale of Perfection*, 100.

[108] Hilton, 101.

[109] Hilton, 101.

[110] Hilton, 103.

[111] Hilton, 105.

[112] Hilton, 104.

[113] Hilton, 231.

[114] Hilton, 96.

[115] Hilton, 220.

[116] Hilton, 79.

[117] Hilton, 80.

[118] Hilton, 82.

[119] Hilton, 223.

[120] Hilton, 123.

[121] Hilton, 123.

RECOMMENDED READING

Primary texts with helpful introductions. Read the mystics for yourself.

Hilton, Walter, *The Scale of Perfection*. Edited by John Clark and Rosemar Dorward (New York: Paulist, 1991).

Hilton, Walter, *Mixed Life*. Translated by Rosemary Dorward (Oxford: SLG Press, 2001).

Rolle, Richard, *The Fire of Love*. Translated by Clifton Wolters (Harmondsworth, Middlesex: Penguin Books, 1972).

Walsh, James ed., *The Cloud of Unknowing* (Mahwah, NJ: Paulist, 1981).

Julian of Norwich, *Revelations of Divine Love*. Translated by Barry Windeatt (Oxford: Oxford University Press, 2015).

Kempe, Margery, *The Book of Margery Kempe*. Translated by Barry Windeatt (London: Penguin Classics, 2019).

Devotional texts. To pray over and ponder

Llewelyn, Robert ed., *Enfolded in Love: Daily Readings with Julian of Norwich* (London: Darton, Longman and Todd, 2019).

Llewelyn, Robert, ed., *The Dart of Longing Love: Daily Readings from the Cloud of Unknowing* (London: Darton, Longman and Todd, 2004).

Goodrich, Kevin, *The Greatest Desire: Daily Readings with Walter Hilton* (London: Darton, Longman and Todd, 2023).

More on the English Mystics

Nuth, Joan M., *God's Lovers in an Age of Anxiety: The Medieval English Mystics* (London: Darton, Longman and Todd, 2001).

Make your Pilgrimage

Mayhew-Smith, Nick, and Hayward, Guy, *Britain's Pilgrim Places: The First Complete Guide to Every Spiritual Treasure* (London: Lifestyle Press, 2020).

APPENDIX B

STARTING POINTS FOR ACADEMIC STUDY

I n addition to the texts referenced in the main body of this book and in the last two reference sections, the following works may be helpful to those doing academic work in the areas of Christian theology and spirituality. Think of these as starting points into a forest of scholars and texts. Students will want to research newer publications as well as the many excellent older ones.

Mysticism

Lamm, Julia A. ed., *The Wiley Blackwell Companion to Christian Mysticism* (Oxford: Blackwell Publishing, 2013).

Christian Spirituality

Dryer, Elizabeth, and Burrows, Mark S., eds., *The Study of Christian Spirituality* (Baltimore, Maryland: John Hopkins University Press, 2005).

Hilton and the English Mystics

Chappell, Arthur, 'Walter Hilton: A Contemplative Spirituality for All the Baptized', *Downside Review* 113, no. 390 (1995): 36–53.

APPENDIX B

Clark, John, 'Action and Contemplation in Walter Hilton', *Downside Review* 97, no. 329 (1979): 258–74.

Clark, Patrick M. '"Feeling" in Walter Hilton's *The Scale of Perfection*', *Downside Review* 127, no. 446 (2009): 23–48.

Fanous, Samuel, and Gillespie, Vincent, eds., *The Cambridge Companion to Medieval English Mysticism* (Cambridge, UK: Cambridge University Press, 2011).

Goodrich, Kevin, *Mystic Bonfires: Walter Hilton and the Development of Practical Spiritual Theology* (Eugene, OR: Wipf and Stock, 2022).

Gutgsell, Jessie, 'The Gift of Tears: Weeping in the Religious Imagination of Western Medieval Christianity', *Anglican Theological Review* 97, no. 2 (2015): 239–53.

Jones, E.A., ed., *The Medieval Mystical Tradition in England: Exeter Symposium VIII* (Cambridge: D.S. Brewer, 2013).

Riehle, Wolfgang, *The Secret Within: Hermits, Recluses, and Spiritual Outsiders in Medieval England* (Ithaca, New York: Cornell University, 2014).

Ringer, Jeffrey, 'Faith and Language: Walter Hilton, St Augustine and Poststructural Semiotics', *Christianity and Literature* 53, no. 1 (2003): 3–18.

Ross, Ellen, 'Submission or Fidelity: The Unity of Church and Mysticism in Walter Hilton's *Scale of Perfection*', *Downside Review* 106, no. 363 (1988): 134–144.

APPENDIX C

CELEBRATE THE ENGLISH MYSTICS

On your own, with family and friends, at your local church, and with others celebrate the feast days of these saints as observed by The Church of England.

Richard Rolle – 20 January

Walter Hilton – 24 March

Julian of Norwich – 8 May

Margery Kempe – 9 November

The Episcopal Church in the United States celebrates Richard Rolle, Walter Hilton, and Margery Kempe on 9 November.

LITURGICAL MATERIALS FOR HILTON'S FEAST DAY

for use on Walter Hilton's Feast Day, 24 March, and other appropriate occasions.

Walter Hilton of Thurgarton
Mystic, Canon, 1396

Walter Hilton is one of a small group of fourteenth-century mystics that comprise a period in the history of spirituality sometimes called the 'Golden Age of English Mysticism'. Julian of Norwich, another mystic associated with this 'golden age' was a near contemporary of Hilton. It appears she was familiar with some of his ideas. Hilton's writings on prayer and the spiritual life were immensely influential in England in the fourteenth and fifteenth centuries. Hilton was read by laity and clergy, as well as those in monasteries. His most famous works are *The Scale of Perfection,* where he provides spiritual direction to an anchoress and *The Mixed Life,* where Hilton is addressing the situation of a man of influence with familial and professional responsibilities.

Hilton was born around the year 1340. Little is known about his early life. Later he studied canon law at Cambridge. Eventually, he abandoned the practice of law in order to dedicate his life to prayer, devotion, and contemplation. This eventually led him to join the community of Augustinian Canons in the village of Thurgarton, not far from Southwell. He died there on the eve of the Annunciation on March 24 in the year 1396. In the *Scale of Perfection* he writes, 'For what is a man but his thoughts and loves?' Hilton's spiritual guidance encourages careful self-reflection as well as a cultivation of a holy desire to experience more of the love of God. In the *Mixed Life* Hilton writes, 'The more desire that you have toward him, the more is this fire of love within you.' Hilton quotes Hebrews 12:29 to explain: 'For our God is a consuming fire.'

In addition to the above, one or more passages from this volume may be read. Alternatively, selected passages from The Greatest Desire: Daily Readings with Walter Hilton *may be read.*

Collect:

Almighty God, Holy Trinity, thou didst reveal to thy servant, Walter Hilton, thine mysteries of perfect love, may we, following his example, find our faith kindled with fire and our spiritual eyes opened to thy glory, through Jesus Christ our Lord, the lover of our souls, who liveth and reigneth with thee and the Holy Spirit one God, now and ever. Amen.

or

Almighty God, Holy Trinity, you revealed to your servant, Walter Hilton, the mysteries of your perfect love, may we, following his example, find our faith kindled with fire and our spiritual eyes opened to your glory, through Jesus Christ our Lord, the lover of our souls, who lives and reigns with you and the Holy Spirit, one God, now and forever. Amen.

Post Communion:

Almighty God, who graciously made us according to thy image, by the power of thy Holy Spirit reform us in faith and

APPENDIX D

feeling, that we, having celebrated the mysteries of thy Son's Body and Blood, may like thy servant Walter Hilton, grow in thy grace and abound in thy love. Amen.

or

Almighty God, who graciously made us according to your image, by the power of your Holy Spirit reform us in faith and feeling, that we, having celebrated the mysteries of your Son's Body and Blood, may like your servant Walter Hilton, grow in your grace and abound in your love. Amen.

Psalm	Lessons
46	Genesis 1:26-27; Ephesians 3:14-21; Luke 10:38-42

Optional Hymns

Jerusalem the Golden

Jerusalem my Happy Home

I Know Not Where the Road Will Lead

Love Divine All Loves Excelling

PILGRIMAGE TO THE LANDS OF HILTON

Walter Hilton lived, ministered, and died as a member of the Augustinian priory in Thurgarton. The existing building, on the site of the original priory, includes architectural elements from Hilton's time in the fourteenth century. The Priory Church of St Peter is a beautiful historic church, located in a peaceful and idyllic setting. There is a memorial to Walter Hilton on one of the pillars in the nave, done by a local artist as part of a celebration marking the 600th anniversary of Hilton's death in 1996. This rendition of Hilton is suitable for those wishing to mark their visit to the holy place by 'taking a picture' with the saint who once worshipped within the church's walls. The priory church is accessible from the main road, about five minutes by car from Southwell. It is recommended to make the pilgrimage to the priory church by foot. This can be done from Southwell Minster, by taking walking paths through lovely pastoral landscapes.

Maps are available online from the British Pilgrimage Trust. Contact the vicar of St Peter's for access to the interior of the church. Pilgrims may wish to stay or visit Sacrista Prebend. Sacrista Prebend is a retreat house in Southwell, across from the Minster. Sacrista has helped to keep Hilton's witness alive in many ways, including by naming a room after him. The Minster was founded around the year 1000. In 1884 the Minster became the cathedral of the local Anglican diocese and today is the cathedral for the Diocese of Southwell and Nottingham. In the fourteenth century, the Minster, like the Priory in Thurgarton, was a significant centre. It is likely Hilton made the hour walk to the Minster on more than one occasion during his years in Thurgarton. The walking pilgrimage can be done in either direction. Visitors are encouraged to begin or conclude their journey in one of the chapels or altars in the Minster. The Minster gift shop and cafe is nearby.

A Prayer for Making Pilgrimage to Thurgarton

Almighty God, who inspires the desires of *our* hearts to embrace the pilgrim's way. Protect and inspire us during our journey. Bring us to that quiet place in the village of Thurgarton where Walter Hilton lived, ministered, and died. May the fire of your love kindle our faith, assuage our doubts, and grant us guidance about the matters that occupy our minds. When *we* have finished this portion of our earthy pilgrimage, strengthen us for the roads ahead, through Jesus Christ our Lord, who is Himself, our final pilgrimage, the true Jerusalem, who lives and reigns with you and the Holy Spirit, one God, now and forever. Amen.

APPENDIX F

KINDLING CONTEMPLATION IN VARIOUS SETTINGS

These ideas are brief, provisional, and incomplete. They are intended to spark your imagination. You are best positioned, with others seeking Jerusalem, to flesh these ideas out, improve them, and come up with your own ideas and then implement them in your life and local communities.

In the Home
Have devotional objects visible (e.g., Bible, Prayerbook, cross, etc.), consider having a prayer corner, home altar, or icon wall. Think of your home as your anchorhold.

Regularly disengage from technology, allow for periods of silence.

Among Friends
Make a local pilgrimage together. It could be to a historic church, a retreat centre, a monastery, or a natural place of wonder and beauty. Eat together. Laugh together. Walk in silence together.

Pray for your friends, for their needs and concerns, but also for their relationship with God.

APPENDIX F

In Marriage

Pray together regularly, it could be before 'lights out' at night or in the morning.

Engage together in the works of spiritual and corporal mercy, perhaps finding a regular opportunity to do so (e.g., soup kitchen, building a friendship with a neighbour who needs your help, volunteering, etc.)

With Children

Introduce them to the Bible, the saints and mystics through artwork and through story.

Teach them the traditional prayers (e.g., 'Our Father') or simple prayers (e.g., I thank you God for ...). These prayers will remain with them for the rest of their lives.

In Local Churches

Create spaces in worship and at other times for silence.

Start prayer groups and try to encourage robust teaching on the spiritual life, including in sermons.

In Theological Education

Have every student spend time at a monastery or retreat centre, at least once a term/semester.

Weave prayer (vocal, liturgical, and silent) into the daily schedule and into every class.

APPENDIX 6

SLICES FOR MEDITATION

These quotations are intended for your meditation. Take a moment, take longer, return to them, leave them behind, and then come back to them again.

'Love God less and you love everyone and everything less.'

Bishop Rowan Williams,
Being Disciples: Essentials of the Christian Life

'There is one useful and deserving task on which to labour, a plain highway to contemplation, as far as can lie in human effort: and that is for a person to go into themselves and know their own soul and its powers, its fairness and its foulness.'

Walter Hilton, *The Scale of Perfection*

'The most important part of prayer technique is to keep at it, to give it a daily place in our lives. Even a quarter hour a day is better than a prayer binge now and then. If we are faithful to a daily amount of prayer, we will want to pray at other times during the day, in our various needs and activities. But we must withdraw some time each day from those needs and activities, from the making of our world. Even if the prayer time seems to be no more than a refined nuisance, it is giving life to the rest of our day.'

Sister Miriam Pollard OCSO, *The Laughter of God*

APPENDIX G

'Sometimes we don't need another chance to express how we feel or to ask someone to understand our situation. Sometimes we just need a firm kick in the pants. An unsmiling expectation that if we mean all these wonderful things we talk about and sing about, then let's see something to prove it.'

Dietrich Bonhoeffer, *The Cost of Discipleship*

'Our Lord Jesus often said, "It is I. It is I. It is I who am highest. It is I you love. It is I you delight in. It is I you serve. It is I you long for. It is I you desire. It is I who am your purpose. It is I who am all. It is I that Holy Church preaches and teaches you. It is I who showed myself to you here."'

Julian of Norwich, *Revelations of Divine Love*

'It is much easier to pray for a bore than to go visit him.'

C. S. Lewis, *Letters to Malcolm: Chiefly on Prayer*

'Any way that we can improve and enrich human life is living the Christian life, and every way in which we enjoy and appreciate what is good and beautiful can be an act of obedience.'

Diogenes Allen, *Spiritual Theology:*
The Theology of Yesterday for Spiritual Help Today

USING THIS BOOK IN VARIOUS SETTINGS

For small groups, classes, and churches.
This book is best explored by a group over a period of at least five weeks. The five-chapter format lends itself to use during Lent (finishing the book prior to Holy Week or leaving the conclusion for Holy Week), but the book can be used at any time of the year.

The end-of-chapter materials can be assigned or encouraged and then discussed.

Groups or classes wanting to read through entire or large selections of the five mystics writings can use this book as an organizing structure or an introduction to the material.

For example:

Introduction

Chapter 1

Chapter 2

Chapter 3 + Primary writings (*The Fire of Love, The Cloud of Unknowing*)

Chapter 4 + Primary writings (*Revelations of Divine Love, Book of Margery Kempe*)

APPENDIX H

Chapter 5 + Primary writings (*The Scale of Perfection, The Mixed Life*)

Conclusion

Retreats, Quiet Days, and Days of Reflection

The book could be used to structure a retreat, quiet day, or day of reflection. The chapters could be read during periods of silence and then discussed in common. Alternatively, five presentations could be made, following the general topics of the five chapters, with group reflection happening silently or aloud by listeners.

In Spiritual Direction

The book could be read in its entirety and discussed at the start or end of a session. Alternatively, it could be discussed at a separate time, apart from direction itself.

It could also be discussed, as an opening devotional, over a series of sessions.

This book could also serve as a fruitful study for the initial training or ongoing formation of spiritual directors and others, such as clergy, involved in giving spiritual guidance.

APPENDIX I

JERUSALEM THE GOLDEN

Jerusalem the Golden   HEAVEN

Words: Bernard of Cluny, 1146. Translated by John Mason Neale, 1858.
Music: 'Ewing' Alexander C. Ewing, 1853. Setting: "Hymns Ancient and Modern", 1861.
copyright: public domain. This score is a part of the Open Hymnal Project, 2010 Revision.

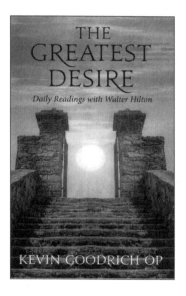

ENFOLDED IN LOVE

Daily Readings of Love, Forgiveness and Joy

Julian of Norwich

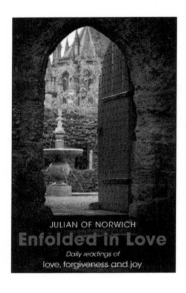

Order from www.dltbooks.com or contact
Norwich Books and Music at
orders@norwichbooksandmusic.com
or on 01603 785925

DARTON·LONGMAN+TODD

INTELLIGENT ♦ INSPIRATIONAL ♦ INCLUSIVE
SPIRITUAL BOOKS

IN SEARCH OF JULIAN OF NORWICH

Sheila Upjohn

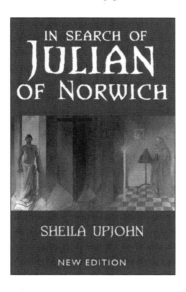

Order from www.dltbooks.com or contact
Norwich Books and Music at
orders@norwichbooksandmusic.com
or on 01603 785925

DARTON · LONGMAN + TODD

INTELLIGENT ◆ INSPIRATIONAL ◆ INCLUSIVE
SPIRITUAL BOOKS

GOD'S LOVERS IN AN AGE OF ANXIETY

The Medieval English Mystics

Julian of Norwich

Order from www.dltbooks.com or contact
Norwich Books and Music at
orders@norwichbooksandmusic.com
or on 01603 785925

DARTON·LONGMAN +TODD

INTELLIGENT ♦ INSPIRATIONAL ♦ INCLUSIVE
SPIRITUAL BOOKS